Decisions Made Now Will Benefit Y⸺

We all r
them m
A safe ar
knowledg⸺   ⸺.⸺ial advisor,
ask the ric⸺   ⸺ proactive role in your
retirement ⸺ ⸺y.

It is important to work with a financial advisor who is aware of the latest IRA distribution and tax rules, including the major changes made by the 2019 retirement plan law (the SECURE Act). These rules are complicated and full of tax traps that could cost you your retirement dreams. If our current economic situation has taught us anything, choosing an educated financial advisor is essential to keeping more of your hard-earned money.

I do not sell investment products. I do not earn commissions. I simply believe that a comfortable retirement starts with accurate IRA advice. I am here to educate. That is the message behind this guide, which will provide you with 125 essential ways to save your wealth so that you can spend your golden years how you have planned and envisioned them.

No one knows for sure what 2021 will bring, so as always, go to my website **irahelp.com** to find out the latest information and any other major tax rule changes that could affect your retirement savings.

I hope you find my *Retirement Decisions Guide* educational and useful.

Ed Slott, CPA
Ed Slott and Company, LLC

Copyright © 2021 by IRAHelp, LLC
All rights reserved

Cover and interior design by Debbie Slott
dslottdesign.com

Cover photo © Christian Wheatley

NOTE: This guide is designed to provide accurate and authoritative information with respect to the subject matter covered. It is not a substitute for customized financial advice suitable for your needs, goals and risk tolerance. If you require customized financial advice or other personalized assistance, you should seek the services of a competent professional.

CONTENTS

Chapter 1:

IRA Basics

1. Plan now and retire twice as rich

Studies show that people who become educated about their finances and play a role in planning and monitoring their IRAs wind up twice as rich as those who haven't a clue. Consider these three facts from a Dartmouth/Wharton study:

- **Wisdom pays**—Retirement planning is a strong predictor of retirement wealth. If you learn how money grows and how much you will need at retirement, you are much more likely to achieve your stated goals.

- **Money grows**—Those who plan are more likely to end up at retirement with twice the wealth of those who do not plan.

- **Start early**—Those who are financially literate when young are more likely to plan for retirement.

2. Avoid past years' mistakes

The Great Recession and the pandemic were painful for most IRA investors. But these valuable lessons were learned:

- **Get IRA advice.** If you are unsure what to do, consider hiring a financial advisor who understands IRA portfolio allocation, tax issues, diversification, distribution planning, hedging and emotional handholding.

- **Keep some cash.** Setting cash aside in your IRA will buffer your portfolio against downturns and let you invest when share prices are low.

- **Know your mix.** Proper allocation among stocks and bonds—and diversification among different stock and bond classes—is essential.

- **Stocks aren't certain.** Stocks are volatile, and stock-price growth comes after long periods of time. Even after 15 years, stock values can suddenly decline or remain flat for a period. Ease volatility by investing in a strategic mix of assets—such as stocks, bonds, annuities, cash, real estate and other investments.

- **Bonds have risks.** Many investors shooting for income continue to invest in individual bonds. But as we know now, any company—including "safe" ones—can go belly-up. That's why bond investments need to be highly diversified among many different types of fixed-income securities, through bond funds or individual bonds.

- **Market cycles end.** Both rising and declining markets have to be planned for and taken advantage of. The market has always gone in cycles. While a severe market downturn can cause financial anxiety, it will eventually end. But it can also be capitalized on with buying opportunities.

3. What are the IRA rules for 2021?

Contribution Levels

- **Up through age 49—**$6,000 for 2021 or your taxable compensation for the year, whichever is lower.
  (Visit **irahelp.com/2021** for all 2021 IRA and tax tables.)

- **Age 50 onward—**$7,000 for 2021 or your taxable compensation for the year, whichever is lower.
  (Visit **irahelp.com/2021** for all 2021 IRA and tax tables.)

Conversion Eligibility

- **Everyone qualifies** to convert a traditional IRA or SEP IRA to a Roth IRA. After a two-year waiting period, SIMPLE IRAs can also be converted. Income restrictions on a conversion were repealed starting in 2010.

4. Do these myths sound familiar?

Many people who don't save enough in a 401(k) and IRA typically have five reasons why not. But those feel-good excuses are flawed. Here's why:

- **Myth: Taxes will be lower.** Many people believe that when they retire, their tax rates will be lower because they won't be earning as much income. But there's nothing stopping the government from raising them in future years. So withdrawals from a traditional IRA years from now could actually face higher income taxes—even if you're not working.

- **Myth: You'll work longer.** When portfolios were down, many people shrugged and said they'll just have to work longer. Sounds good, but here's a stark fact: As you age, the odds are you physically won't be able to work as hard as you want—or as long as you once did.

- **Myth: Pensions will kick in.** As we know now, even companies that may once have been healthy sometimes end up filing for bankruptcy. Or restructure. Or face such hardships that they roll back benefits they once promised. This can include government and public pensions that were once thought to be secure.

- **Myth: Social Security starts at 62.** That's true—now. But there's nothing to say that the federal government won't raise the minimum age at which benefits start—or reduce benefits for those at specific income levels.

- **Myth: Inheritances will arrive.** Don't count on it. Many seniors are living longer today thanks to dietary changes and moderate exercise. Even when aging adults grow ill, medical care is so good that infirmities can be controlled and minimized for years. Lucky you—mom and dad will live forever!

5. Why bother saving in an IRA?

If you're contributing to a 401(k) at work, you may be wondering why you need an Individual Retirement Account (IRA). Or you may feel you can't afford to save the max in both. But opening and saving even a little in an IRA is important. Here's why:

- **Tax-free growth.** Assets in an IRA grow tax-free—meaning there are no taxes on capital gains when you sell assets within the account. Taxes are paid upon distribution.

- **Tax deduction.** You can always deduct your full traditional IRA contribution if your modified adjusted gross income in 2021 is less than $105,000 (married filing jointly) or $66,000 (single) (visit **irahelp.com/2021** for all 2021 IRA and tax tables).

- **Investment freedom.** Unlike a 401(k), which typically offers a small menu of mutual funds, an IRA lets you invest in any securities you wish. In addition, you can use an IRA to diversify your total retirement portfolio by investing in assets not offered by your 401(k).

- **Long-range planning.** When you eventually leave your job, you will almost certainly wind up transferring the balance of your 401(k) into an IRA for greater investment choices, control and efficiency. You may as well open one now, even if you don't contribute the max each year.

6. What is a traditional IRA?

The Individual Retirement Account (IRA) was created in 1974 with the enactment of the Employee Retirement Income Security Act (ERISA). The original version is commonly called a "traditional IRA," which distinguishes it from other types of IRAs that have been introduced over the years. What you need to know about a traditional IRA:

- **Contributions.** Each year you may contribute up to an amount set by the tax law—provided you or your spouse earned at least that sum in salary or self-employment income (i.e., compensation). The max you can contribute is based on whether you are age 49 or younger—or age 50 or older. Before 2020, contributions could not be made once you reached the year you turned age 70½. The 2019 retirement plan law (the SECURE Act) lifted that age restriction so that traditional IRA contributions for 2020 and subsequent years can be made at any age. (Visit **irahelp.com/2021** for current levels.)

- **Deadline.** Annual contributions can be made until April 15 of the following year.
- **Deduction.** If you are covered by a company plan, you can deduct your annual contribution if you meet the latest income levels (visit **irahelp.com/2021** for the current levels).
- **Gains.** Gains on assets in an IRA are not taxed until they are withdrawn, giving assets an enormous opportunity to compound and grow over time.
- **Withdrawals.** The traditional IRA was created to encourage retirement savings. So, withdrawals before age 59½ face both income tax and a stiff 10% penalty. You can withdraw penalty-free starting at age 59½—but withdrawals aren't mandatory. Starting at age 72, you are required to take annual distributions based on the IRS' life-expectancy table.
- **Taxes.** Withdrawals face income taxes at your tax rate at the time.
- **Heirs.** The person or persons you want to receive your assets upon death should be named in your IRA beneficiary document. IRA assets shouldn't be passed through your will.

7. What is a Roth IRA?

The Roth IRA was named for William Roth, a U.S. senator from Delaware who sponsored the Taxpayer Relief Act of 1997. Here's what you need to know:

- **Qualifications.** Only taxpayers under specific income levels can open and contribute annually to a Roth IRA (visit **irahelp.com/2021** for the latest qualifying levels).
- **Contributions.** Each year you may contribute up to an amount set by the tax law, provided you earned at least that sum in salary or self-employment income. The max you can contribute is based

on whether you are age 49 or younger—or age 50 or older (visit **irahelp.com/2021** for the latest levels). Annual contributions can be made at any age.

- **Deadline.** Annual contributions can be made up until April 15 of the following year.

- **Deduction.** There is no tax deduction for contributions to a Roth IRA.

- **Gains.** Gains on assets in a Roth IRA are generally not taxed, giving them an enormous opportunity to grow and compound over time.

- **Withdrawals.** Assets in a Roth IRA may be withdrawn after age 59½ tax-free if any Roth was opened more than five years earlier. That means every dollar growing in a Roth IRA can be yours to keep. In addition, there is no mandatory withdrawal age, meaning assets can continue to grow tax-free.

- **Penalty.** Gains withdrawn before age 59½ will face a 10% penalty plus taxation. Certain pre-59 ½ distributions of converted funds also face a 10% penalty.

- **Heirs.** The person or persons you want to receive your assets upon death should be named in your Roth IRA's beneficiary document. Roth IRA assets shouldn't be passed through your will.

- **Inheritance.** Upon death, a Roth IRA can pass estate-tax free to a spouse. Or it can pass to one or more non-spousal beneficiaries, though part of the assets may be needed to pay estate taxes. For deaths in 2020 or subsequent years, most non-spouse heirs must receive the entire distribution by December 31 of the tenth year after the owner's death. (See tips #109-111.) But the required annual distributions are generally income-tax free. The catch is that a Roth IRA had to have been set up by the original Roth IRA owner more than five years before the distribution.

8. What is a SEP IRA?

A Simplified Employee Pension Individual Retirement Account (SEP IRA) is an IRA for the self-employed or small-business owner. The rules for a SEP IRA are the same as for a traditional IRA (see tip #6)—with the following exceptions:

- **To qualify.** Although available to businesses of any size, a SEP IRA is generally used by a self-employed individual or small-business owner. You can open a SEP IRA even if you work for an employer and participate in another retirement plan—provided your side business generates income and complies with certain ownership guidelines.

- **Contributions.** You can contribute up to 20% of net earnings from self-employment—(25% of wages, if incorporated)—but not to exceed annual amounts set by the tax law (visit **irahelp.com/2021** for the latest levels). If your business has employees, all eligible employees must receive the same benefits under a SEP IRA plan.

- **Taxes.** Contributions are deductible dollar for dollar. This means if you contribute $25,000 to your SEP IRA, you can deduct this amount from your income on tax returns. This feature makes SEP IRA contributions highly desirable from a retirement-planning and tax-savings standpoint.

9. Which IRA is right for you?

- **What's your income?** If your income level is under the eligibility threshold, open a Roth IRA.

- **Are you self-employed?** Open a SEP IRA and contribute up to 20% of your net income (25% if you're incorporated)—but not more than the annual amounts set by the tax law (visit **irahelp.com/2021** for the latest levels).

- **Do you have kids?** Open a Roth IRA for teens with salaried summer jobs. You can make the contributions on their behalf. So, if your child earned $2,000 over the summer, you can contribute up to that amount in his or her Roth IRA. They will thank you when they retire and can withdraw the accumulated assets tax-free.

10. Easy way to save $32,000

You can easily contribute at least $1,326 a year to an IRA. Here's how: The average American winds up with $5.50 in spare change each week. Pool the coins along with $20 per week in stray singles, and you'll have $1,326 by year's end. Why bother? If you continue to contribute this sum annually for 15 years, and your IRA account earns a modest 6% annually on a compounded basis, you will wind up with nearly $32,000. That's hardly chump change.

11. What is a Roth IRA conversion?

The tax code lets you convert all or part of your traditional IRA or SEP IRA to a Roth IRA. Prior to 2010, the tax code allowed such a conversion—but only if your annual income did not exceed $100,000. But starting in 2010, this income threshold was repealed. That means anyone can convert a traditional IRA into a Roth IRA—regardless of annual income. What you need to know:

- **Benefit:** A Roth conversion grants you all the benefits of a Roth IRA—including tax-free withdrawals of earnings after five years of ownership and after reaching age 59½.

- **Drawback:** You must pay income tax on the portfolio's market value on the date of conversion.

12. Does a Roth IRA conversion pay?

In many cases, the answer is a resounding yes. If you can pay the income tax due on the portfolio's market value at the time of conversion, the move is a powerful one.

- **Here's why:** Historically, today's income-tax rates are relatively low. A conversion allows you to pay income tax at the current rate and get rid of Uncle Sam for life. So, for example, if a $500,000 portfolio in a Roth IRA grows to $1 million in 15 years, all of those dollars are yours. And you get to enjoy all of the benefits of a Roth IRA, including no mandatory withdrawals.

13. Roth IRA conversion questions

Converting your traditional IRA to a Roth IRA is a terrific deal. Anyone can do this—regardless of annual income, but you will owe income tax on the conversion. Five big questions:

- **When doesn't it pay?** If you expect your income to decline in retirement and tax rates to be where they are now, a Roth conversion might not be ideal. That's because the tax hit on your withdrawals from a traditional IRA in the future will likely be lower than what you would have to pay now to convert.

- **How is a conversion taxed?** If you convert part or all of a traditional IRA to a Roth IRA, you will owe income tax on the assets' market value on the date of conversion. But if you have made nondeductible IRA contributions, you have to follow the IRS' pro-rata tax rule, which can be tricky. Consult a financial advisor or an accountant with specialized knowledge in this area.

- **How to cover the tax?** Ideally you want to use funds in taxable accounts to pay the tax. It doesn't make sense to tap an IRA or 401(k) to pay taxes and a 10% early-withdrawal penalty if you're under age 59½.

- **Can the tax be minimized?** Sure. Convert only part of the traditional IRA.

- **What about a SEP IRA?** Yes, you can convert part or all of a SEP IRA. If you convert the entire SEP IRA, however, you can't continue making deductible contributions to your newly created Roth IRA. Instead, you'll have to set up a new SEP IRA account for future deductible contributions.

Getting tax-free income from a Roth IRA can be rewarding, but getting there from a traditional IRA conversion can be daunting. You'll probably owe income tax on most or all of the retirement funds you convert.

What's more, a complete conversion will often push you into a higher tax bracket. For example, consider Andrew and Bonnie, who are married and file a joint tax return. During her career, Bonnie worked at a series of companies with 401(k) plans.

Whenever Bonnie would change jobs, she'd roll the 401(k) balance into her traditional IRA. By the time the couple reached their 50s, eyeing retirement, there was $250,000 in Bonnie's IRA.

- **Their plan:** Convert Bonnie's traditional IRA to a Roth IRA. However, all of the money in her IRA came from pre-tax 401(k) contributions. A complete rollover would add $250,000 to Bonnie and Andrew's taxable income for the year.

  Typically, their taxable income (after deductions) is around $120,000 a year. That puts them in the 22% tax bracket.

  Another $250,000 in taxable income from a Roth IRA conversion would push them all the way through the 22% and 24% brackets, well into the 32% bracket. They might owe about $62,000 in additional federal income tax.

- **Going partial:** Instead, Bonnie decides to convert only $25,000 of her IRA this year. That would increase the couple's taxable income to $145,000, still within the 22% tax bracket for 2021. The added tax would be $5,500 (22% of $25,000), which Andrew and Bonnie can manage. Bonnie plans to implement partial Roth IRA conversions year after year, staying within a tax bracket to hold down the tax bill. Eventually, her entire traditional IRA will be moved to the Roth side, at a relatively low tax cost over a period of years.

- **Ed Slott's advice:** A series of partial conversions will make it easier to pay the tax from a taxable account. Then your entire traditional IRA can become a Roth IRA without a haircut for withdrawals to pay the tax bill.

14. Yes, current tax rates are low

Federal income tax rates are at historic lows. Even if you're paying a top federal rate of 37%, your rate is relatively low and may rise to pay for the new wave of Congressional spending and deficits. (For a look at the 2021 tax rates, see Chapter 8.) Over time, the top tax rate has been as high as 94%. Remember, Congress can change the tax rates at any time for all taxpayers or just for those who earn more than a specific level.

Year	Top Federal Income Tax Rate
2018 - 2021	37%
2013 - 2017	39.6%
2003 - 2012	35%
2002	38.6%
2001	39.1%
1993 - 2000	39.6%
1991 - 1992	31%
1988 - 1990	28%
1987	38.5%
1982 - 1986	50%
1965 - 1981	70%
1964	77%
1954 - 1963	91%
1952 - 1953	92%
1946 - 1951	91%
1944 - 1945	94%

15. What's a recharacterization?

A recharacterization is a way to undo Traditional or Roth IRA contributions. In the past, this strategy could also be used to undo Roth IRA conversions. However, the Tax Cuts and Jobs Act (passed in December 2017) eliminated recharacterizations for Roth IRA conversions that took place after December 31, 2017. As a result, while you can still recharacterize a contribution, Roth IRA conversions are now irrevocable.

- **How it works:** Let's say you checked all the rules and determined you were eligible to open a Roth IRA. You went ahead and opened the account and began making contributions to the

Roth IRA. However, in that same year you received a promotion that came with a significant raise. Because of the added income, you are no longer eligible to make Roth IRA contributions. Under the tax law, your contributions are now subject to a tax penalty. Basically, you just got penalized for doing great work. Not fair!

- **Solution:** You can recharacterize the Roth IRA contributions to a traditional IRA. Whether the contributions are deductible in the IRA is going to depend on your income and whether you or your spouse are covered by a retirement plan at work. You would have to file Form 8606 with your income tax return to report any non-deductible contributions.

16. Who's your IRA beneficiary?

No matter what kind of IRA you own, request a copy of your signed beneficiary form for review. When you receive it, be sure that the people you want to inherit your IRA's assets are listed properly. Also provide your advisor and estate attorney with copies of the signed document.

- **Reason:** When you die, your IRA does not pass according to wishes in your will. Whatever IRA assets are left will pass to the person or persons named in your signed beneficiary document.

17. Inheriting an IRA: Spouse

Under the tax law, if you inherit a spouse's IRA, there are generally no estate or income taxes due—no matter how large your inheritance. But you have three choices regarding how to treat the IRA inheritance:

- **Option #1: You can roll** the inherited IRA assets into your existing IRA or one you set up in your own name.

- **Option #2: You can transfer** the inherited IRA assets into an Inherited IRA account. If your spouse was age 72 or older, you must begin taking mandatory distributions by December 31 of the year following your spouse's death. If your spouse was younger than age 72, you can delay distributions until your spouse would have turned age 72.

- **Option #3: You can disclaim** all or part of the IRA inheritance within nine months of the IRA owner's death. You do not get to choose who is next in line to receive the disclaimed property. Instead, the assets will pass to the IRA's contingent beneficiary, as if you had died before the IRA's owner. Since the assets will be passing to a non-spouse, estate taxes may be owed based on the value of the IRA.

18. Inheriting an IRA: Non-spouse

If you inherit an IRA from a parent or someone who isn't your spouse, you have three choices:

- **Option #1: Take distributions.** Whether you inherit a traditional IRA or a Roth IRA, you cannot roll the assets into your existing IRA as a non-spouse. Instead, you must set up an "Inherited IRA" and have the assets transferred directly in there. Rules…

  1. For deaths in 2020 or subsequent years, most non-spouse beneficiaries must take their entire account by December 31 of the tenth year following the IRA owner's death.

  2. If you are an "eligible designated beneficiary" (see tip #110), begin taking minimum distributions from the Inherited IRA by December 31 of the year following the IRA owner's death. Minimum annual withdrawals are based on the IRS' Single Life Expectancy Table (visit **irahelp.com/2021** to view the IRS table).

- **Option #2: Take the total.** You can choose to take the full value of the inherited IRA as a lump-sum check. You will owe income tax on the sum if you inherited a non-spousal traditional IRA. If you inherited a Roth IRA, you may owe income tax on earnings if the owner did not have any Roth IRA for at least five years.

- **Option #3: Disclaim it.** Your third option is to disclaim the inheritance within nine months of the IRA owner's death. Why would you do this? In most cases it's done to pass the inheritance to the next-in-line beneficiary who may need it more than you do. Either way, upon inheriting, you should immediately name heirs on the beneficiary form.

- **Ed Slott's advice:** Consult an IRA advisor on the appropriate choice. If you take distributions or a lump sum from an inherited traditional IRA, see if you can claim the IRD deduction ("income in respect of a decedent"). It's a deduction for inheritors of a traditional IRA on which federal estate taxes were paid (see tip #66).

19. Did you inherit a Roth IRA?

- **If you're the spouse**—you can roll the inherited Roth IRA into your existing Roth IRA or a newly set-up Roth IRA in your own name. Then you can avoid taking distributions for life if you choose. You also can retitle the Roth IRA as your own. Either way, upon inheriting, you should immediately name heirs on the beneficiary form. When your heirs inherit from you, they will likely have to take the entire remaining account by December 31 of the tenth year following your death—income-tax free.

- **If you're a non-spouse—**

  1. For deaths in 2020 or subsequent years, most non-spouse beneficiaries must take their entire account by December 31 of the tenth year following the IRA owner's death.

  2. If you are an "eligible designated beneficiary" (see tip #110), begin taking minimum distributions from the inherited Roth IRA by December 31 of the year following the Roth IRA owner's death. Minimum annual withdrawals are based on the IRS' Single Life Expectancy Table (visit **irahelp.com/2021** to view the table). But the mandatory annual required distributions will generally be tax-free.

20. Beware of this costly IRA penalty

If you're a non-spouse who's inheriting a Roth IRA, you have to set up an "Inherited Roth IRA" to receive the assets.

- **Big trap:** Be sure to take the entire account out within 10 years after death or, if you are an "eligible designated beneficiary" (see tip #110), take the required minimum distribution (RMD) each year based on the IRS' life-expectancy table (visit **irahelp.com/2021** to view the table). If you don't take the distributions, you will owe a 50% penalty on each RMD you missed—even though the distribution remains tax-free.

21. What wealthy retirees do right

An IRA is likely to be one of your most valuable assets when you retire. While my wealthiest retired clients differ in net worth and retirement goals—all share similar behavior patterns regarding their IRAs and how they saved over time. Here are their saving secrets:

- **Get real.** Most wealthy clients who retire with sizable IRAs resisted becoming greedy over time. They set goals and maintained retirement portfolio allocations that matched their savings targets and risk tolerance levels over time. They also didn't second-guess their plan—even in 2008 or 2020.

- **React smartly.** If your IRA remains properly allocated and highly diversified based on your age and goals, you have little to fear in terms of market swings. You also want to avoid the urge to invest in hot trends or go to 100% cash in a panic. Both moves often backfire.

- **Seek smart help.** Many of my clients who amassed sizable IRAs by retirement age did so with the help of a professional advisor who was educated in IRAs and tax strategies.

- **Watch carefully.** Studies show that if you plan correctly and track your spending and IRA statements, you are more likely to reach your goals. The reason is simple: If you take an interest in your money, you're more likely to care. And if you care, you're more likely to save more, spend less and invest strategically.

- **Withdraw wisely.** You want to leave assets in an IRA as long as possible—especially in retirement. Tax-deferred savings compound over time and have the best chance of greater growth. For income, you're always better off working part-time or withdrawing from taxable accounts first before tapping into your IRA.

- **Hedge risks.** We all fear unforeseen market mishaps. To guard against the impact of downturns, wealthy retirees take protective steps in their IRA portfolios and other accounts. For example, they set aside enough cash to cover emergencies, take out adequate insurance policies to protect against health and financial blows, and invest in a range of different, highly diversified investments to cushion against market setbacks.

- **Ed Slott's advice:** Most people can live comfortably on much less than they're spending now—if they find ways to spend wisely. Many wealthy retirees are happy with the little things in life and appreciate what they already own. Few overspend on cars, boats, homes or vacations. And when they do spend, they are extremely frugal.

Chapter 2:

Making Plans

22. Saving plenty isn't hopeless

No matter how much you need to save by the time you retire, never feel as though saving annually is hopeless. It's not, and even small amounts add up over time. The reason is the "compounded interest" you'll receive in tax-deferred retirement accounts like an IRA.

- **What's compound interest?** This is interest you earn not only on your initial contribution but also on accumulated amounts earned each year. Let's say you have $1,000 in an IRA investment and it earns 7% in the first year. You'll have $1,070. Now let's say that in the second year, your $1,070 earns 6%. You'll have $1,134. And so on, year after year. That's the power of compound interest.

- **Ed Slott's advice:** Set your annual IRA savings goal early in the year and find ways to reach that goal by setting aside money each week or month. Or consider having your IRA plan automatically withdraw the amount from your bank checking account each month. If the money is removed directly, you're less likely to miss it.

23. How much will you need to save?

This answer depends on how much you'll need each year for living expenses in retirement—or once you stop working full-time. How to estimate your savings goal:

- **Step 1.** Gather last month's bills, ATM slips and credit card receipts. Add them up—but leave out expenses that won't likely exist when you retire, such as college tuitions, mortgage payments, credit card debt, disability insurance premiums, etc.

- **Step 2.** Next, multiply your monthly sum by 12 for an annual total.

- **Step 3.** A dollar today will buy less in the future thanks to rising prices (inflation). So take your current annual total and see what it will be in the year you plan to retire. Use an online inflation calculator.

- **Step 4.** Subtract your estimated annual Social Security benefit and any estimated annual pension and annuity payouts. You can calculate your Social Security benefit at SSA.gov.

- **Step 5.** Now you know roughly how much income you'll need in your first year of retirement. But how many years of this income will be enough? While it's impossible to say with any certainty, you can use a life insurance company's life-expectancy table.

- **Step 6.** Multiply your annual retirement income by your years of life expectancy. The result is a rough estimate of how much you'll need to save by retirement. If it seems high, you'll have to cut back on your post-retirement living expenses. Of course, during retirement your savings will need to be invested properly so it keeps pace with inflation.

- **Step 7.** Clearly your goal is to save at least the amount you calculated. Even better is to save a sum that when invested conservatively at 5% will provide you with what you need each year, allowing you to leave your principal intact and pass as much as possible to heirs.

24. How much risk can you tolerate?

Once you know your estimated retirement age and savings goal, the next step is to evaluate how much risk you can tolerate.

ED SLOTT'S
ELITE
IRA
ADVISOR
GROUP™
Find an advisor
at **irahelp.com**

- **What is risk?** Risk is a fancy word for fear. As we know from the economic turmoil of 2008 and 2020, markets drop, sometimes considerably. When they do, investors grow fearful as their portfolios shrink in value. If your portfolio dropped in 2008 or 2020 and you worried you might not have enough years left until retirement to make back what you lost, you likely were overexposed to stocks and took on too much risk.

- **Is safety risky?** Not investing at all is also risky—particularly if you have 15 years or longer until retirement. If you stick only with conservative investments paying a low rate of return, there's a high risk that your portfolio won't grow to the amount you need.

- **Striking a balance.** Risk is about the odds of being exposed to hardship and fear. Finding the right balance between safety and satisfaction requires a little rational thought. Start by looking at how many years you have left until retirement and what rate of return will satisfy your savings goal.

- **Ed Slott's advice:** The more years remaining until retirement, the more risk your portfolio can take on for a higher rate of return. As for your personal fear factor, that's important, too. Fear should play a cautionary role as you determine an ideal rate of return over time. Fear is only a problem if fear alone dictates your investment strategy.

25. What's your asset allocation?

After you figure out when you plan to retire, how much you'll need to save, and the level of risk you can tolerate, you need to determine the ideal asset allocation of your IRA portfolio. Ideally this exercise should be done with a financial advisor who fully understands how IRAs work and the tax benefits involved.

- **What is asset allocation?** Asset allocation is how you divide your savings among stocks, bonds, cash and other investments. Asset allocation is important for two reasons: By properly allocating savings, you maximize your portfolio's growth potential and minimize the negative impact of market declines.

- **How to allocate.** Your allocation levels will depend on when your savings will be needed and the realistic rate of return you can expect over that time period.

- **What's diversification?** Once you've decided what percentage of your portfolio should be devoted to stocks and bonds, the next step is to create a diversified mix of different types of stocks and bonds. This is done to further minimize portfolio jolts over time.

26. When to rebalance a portfolio

No matter how you allocate and diversify your IRA assets now, the mix you choose is likely to become lopsided after 12 months or even sooner. That's because markets are constantly in flux, changing the values of your investments.

- **Example:** If your allocation is supposed to be 50% stocks and 50% bonds, your investment values could change by year-end. How so? A $1,000 investment today in a stock fund may be worth $1,500 at the end of the year. And $1,000 invested in a bond fund may be worth $800. Therefore, your allocation will no longer be 50%-50%, and it will need to be brought back into line.

- **When to rebalance.** Each year, revisit your IRA portfolio to see if it's still allocated and diversified the way you originally planned. If the allocation is too far off, you will need to rebalance your IRA portfolio either alone or with the assistance of a financial advisor.

- **How to rebalance.** You can rebalance two ways: You can sell your position in stock or bond investments in your IRA that exceed your original allocation and invest the proceeds in positions that are below your target percentages. Or you can invest cash in either stock or bond positions to bring the allocation into line.

27. Risks of do-it-yourself planning

While the media has done a fine job over the past 15 years simplifying investing principles for average investors, some magazines and TV shows have oversimplified retirement planning. It's a highly complex process that requires in-depth knowledge and impartiality. Here's how do-it-yourself planners get into trouble:

- **Tip tipsy**—Without someone qualified to remind you of your investment plan, you're more likely to try to capitalize on someone else's hot tip.

- **Too positive**—People who think positively are often successful in life. But they also can get into hot water with their personal finances and investing. That's because positive thinkers tend to assume that markets and their investments will always rebound. As we witnessed in 2008 and 2020, even the mightiest companies can go under, and markets may not rebound fast enough.

- **Hardly objective**—If you make your own financial and investment decisions without seeking professional advice, you're not going to be objective, no matter how hard you try.

- **Lax on laws**—Educated financial advisors keep up with the tax laws that affect retirement planning. If you make a move on your own without understanding or knowing these laws, you could pay more in taxes or lose out on opportunities.

- **Slow on strategies**—New ways to invest emerge all the time. Unless you're up on the different ways to capitalize on tax loopholes, trusts, insurance, annuities and other products, you may not achieve your retirement objectives.

28. Retirement dreams vs. reality

For years, age 65 was the magic number for retirement. Today and in the future, that age may no longer be quitting time. Plan for age 65 but don't assume that work stops then. The odds are greater that work will stop sooner—or later. Here's why:

- **Sudden retirement.** As we know, many people in their 50s found themselves out of work for the first time in their careers during the recession or the pandemic. What's more, many remained unemployed for a year or longer, forcing families to live on less or dip into their savings. When these people did find employment, the jobs typically paid less than what they had been earning. The lesson: Don't assume you'll be working until age 65 or at the salary you're earning now.

- **Much later retirement.** Work used to mean manual labor, so by age 65 most people were physically tired and in need of a much slower pace. Today, many people earn a living on their computers and love what they do. As a result, they intend to continue earning income well into their 70s—either because they want to or because they need to fund some aspect of their lifestyle or the needs of their children.

- **Ed Slott's advice:** When speculating about your retirement age, don't assume too much. The odds are that retirement will come sooner than you think and that your salary in your 60s and 70s will likely be considerably less than you made in your 40s or early 50s. This is why it's so important that you save as much as possible while you're young.

29. Why a financial advisor is essential

Retirement planning is more than just saving enough money for the years when you'll be working less. There are a wide range of complicated retirement issues that need to be considered, including taxes, estate planning and insurance. To retire comfortably, you need financial help. Here's what a financial advisor who's an expert in IRAs can do for you:

- **Less anxiety.** If you hire the right financial advisor, you'll be less likely to worry day after day about whether you've done enough or too little with your investments. Once you and your advisor create a financial plan, your advisor also will help you stick to it.

- **Reduced tracking.** If an advisor has carefully thought through what you need to do and you've implemented the plan, you're less likely to monitor the Dow Jones Industrial Average or S&P 500 day after day. Those are short-term concerns. Instead, you'll be thinking long-term.

- **Size management.** Your IRA is now (or will be soon) your most valuable asset. A qualified financial advisor is trained to manage portfolios as they grow in size and ensure that different asset categories in your portfolio are allocated properly to achieve your stated goals.

- **Coping with complexity.** IRAs have highly complex tax rules that when maximized can save you or your estate from paying much more than necessary in taxes.

- **Legacy management.** It is the job of your financial advisor, in tandem with an estate attorney and accountant, to smoothly transition IRA assets from one generation to the next, minimizing tax issues and maximizing protection.

- **Laws and loopholes.** No one wants to miss out on tax law changes. Only an educated financial advisor stays up on such changes.

30. How to find the right advisor

If you are serious about planning for retirement, you need a professional financial advisor. Believe it or not, I have found that less than 1% of financial advisors are competent IRA distribution specialists. This means that a vast majority of advisors are not up to speed on IRA distribution rules and are ill-equipped to help you plan using your IRA. Here's how to find the right professional advisor:

- **Stick with certification.** Anyone can call himself or herself a "financial advisor." You want an advisor who at least is subject to professional standards and maintains a level of financial education to meet those standards. These include CFP, CFA, ChFC and CPA. While certification does not guarantee competence, a professional designation does indicate at least a standard of education and accountability.

- **Consider specialties.** Two areas that have a big impact on retirement savings are taxes and insurance coverage. Your advisor should have designations such as CPA (accounting) or CLU (insurance), or have access to experts who do.

- **Focus on knowledge.** A financial advisor should know about the latest IRA rules, including the changes made by the 2019 retirement plan law (the SECURE Act). He or she also should know how to integrate your IRA into your broader retirement and estate planning. An advisor must show he or she is continually being educated in the specialized tax rules surrounding IRA accounts.

31. Questions to ask an advisor

How can you be sure a financial advisor is up to speed on IRA issues? Ask the following questions:

ED SLOTT'S
ELITE
IRA
ADVISOR
GROUP™
Find an advisor
at **irahelp.com**

1. **How** do you keep up to date on IRA rules?
2. **When** did you last attend an IRA training course? Ask to see the course manuals.
3. **Are** you up on the latest tax law changes?
4. **What** do you recommend I do with my lump-sum distribution from my company's retirement plan?
5. **Who** should be my IRA beneficiary?
6. **How** do you keep track of my IRA beneficiary forms?
7. **What** is my life expectancy and what is my required IRA distribution if I inherit an IRA? What about my beneficiary?
8. **What** will happen to my IRA after I die? How should an inherited IRA be titled and what required distributions will a beneficiary have to take under the SECURE Act?
9. **How** will you integrate estate planning into your plans for my IRA?

10. **Who** will you turn to for help when you need clarification on IRA rules, estate planning and insurance? If the person says he or she knows it all and doesn't have to ask anyone—run.

Paying a fair price for advice

Among the questions to ask a prospective advisor, be sure to ask how he or she will be paid. You'll want to pay enough so you get good advice, but you don't want to overpay. Here are the major modes of compensation for financial advisors:

- **Traditional.** In the days when most financial advisors were known as brokers, they generally earned sales commissions. That's still true—many financial professionals depend on transaction fees to earn a living.

  Although commissions often get a bad rap, this model still makes sense for some investors, particularly for those who intend to hold their investments for the long-haul.

- **Percentage plays.** These days, many financial advisors rely upon fees rather than commissions. Among fee structures, the most common is charging a percentage of assets under management.

  Many advisors believe that this arrangement puts them "on the same side of the table" as their clients. They're motivated to increase your $500,000 portfolio to $600,000 because they will earn more. Similarly, they have a strong incentive to minimize any declines in your portfolio value, as that will decrease their fees as well.

  There certainly are good reasons why this arrangement has grown in popularity. Nevertheless, paying an asset management fee is not the best plan for everyone. If you seldom change your investments or you interact with your advisor infrequently, you should ask yourself if the fee you are paying is really worth it.

- **Alternate arrangements.** Other compensation structures include retainers, in which you pay a flat fee for advice during a specific time period, perhaps one year. Some advisors charge by the hour, just as accountants and attorneys commonly bill for their services. You may even find an advisor whose compensation includes some combination of the arrangements mentioned above.

- **Ed Slott's advice:** Don't be reluctant to ask an advisor about compensation. Get a written explanation and read it carefully to make sure you understand what you'll be paying.

  Understand what you'll be getting, too. If you participate in a 401(k) plan, for instance, will that advisor help with those decisions, or will you simply continue what you've been doing? You can expect to pay your advisor in some manner, but you should be confident you'll receive a desirable amount of assistance in return.

32. Is your financial advisor honest?

Just because a financial advisor claims to be certified by a professional organization doesn't mean it's true. In the wake of all the recent financial scandals, it's now clear you have to do a little due diligence on the background of anyone you hire to handle your money.

- **Do it yourself**—Verify that your advisor has actually earned his or her credentials by calling the organizations that award certification. Also confirm with the organization that the advisor continues to satisfy ongoing educational requirements, that complaints have not been filed, and that the advisor has not been disciplined.

- **Hire a pro**—Consider hiring an online background-check firm or agency to verify your advisor's education degrees, any legal cases pending, liens and even dangerous levels of personal debt.

33. Does your advisor speak simply?

One of the most important qualifications of a financial advisor is the ability to explain complex matters simply. No matter whom you hire, eventually that person will be recommending investments for your IRA. If that person is unable to explain what the investment is and the rationale for owning it, you have a big problem.

- **Ed Slott's advice:** Before you hire an advisor, ask him or her to explain a Roth IRA conversion, an annuity or how IRAs are distributed after death. If you cannot understand the explanation, or the advisor seems to grow impatient with your questions, there may be a communication problem and a big red flag.

34. How to manage an advisor

Even if you choose an honest, educated IRA advisor who understands the distribution and tax rules, and can explain them clearly, you still need to manage your advisor. You're the boss. The advisor works for you—just as though you were running a business. Here's how to keep your advisor on his or her toes:

- **Meetings**—For the first year, request that you and your advisor meet quarterly. Before these meetings, ask for an agenda of items to be covered.

- **Communication**—E-mails sent to your advisor should be answered promptly. Phone calls also should be returned promptly.

- **Statements**—If your advisor has invested your assets through several different firms, request a consolidated statement outlining your IRA portfolio.

- **Accountability**—Ask knowledgeable questions about your advisor's recommendations. Don't assume everything your advisor says is right or ideal. Questions about your assets are also likely to keep your advisor on his or her toes.

- **Pro-active**—Your advisor should not simply present you with advice and then wait for you to respond. Good advisors stay on clients to ensure that necessary steps are taken and decisions are made.

- **Education**—How is the advisor keeping up on the latest IRA tax rules? They are always changing.

35. How to hire the right CPA

Eventually you will need an accountant who is up on current tax laws, understands the best strategies to keep you from overpaying your taxes, prepares your tax returns on time, and has the skills or resources to assist you in the event of an audit.

- **Ed Slott's advice:** The best place to begin your search for a CPA is by asking friends and colleagues for recommendations. Just be sure you're not hiring more CPA than you need and that the person is suitable for someone with your net worth.

36. How to hire an estate attorney

Nearly 60% of Americans do not have estate plans—and most people who do, neglect to update them regularly. Without up-to-date estate plans in place, all of your hard work saving for retirement and hopes to preserve your wealth for heirs are at risk.

- **Ed Slott's advice:** Ask your financial advisor or friends and colleagues to recommend an estate attorney. Make sure the person understands IRA inheritance and distribution rules. The attorney also should understand the rules that govern distribution of assets to trust beneficiaries and heirs by trustees and estate plan administrators.

37. How to hire an insurance agent

Life insurance is an essential part of retirement planning. You may ask, "How can a life insurance policy benefit me if it won't pay out until I'm dead and gone?" While life insurance can be used to provide heirs with appropriate assets when you die, policies can also be used to guarantee heirs a specific sum so you can spend down what you've saved without worrying if there will be enough for them.

- **Ed Slott's advice:** When choosing a life insurance agent, look for someone who is independent or works with a top-rated, reputable life insurance company and can work with your financial advisor. In many cases, your financial advisor may already have an established relationship with an agent or can find one for you.

Chapter 3:
Minimizing Risks

38. Why knowledge leads to wealth

By now you may be asking yourself the following question: "If I've hired a financial advisor, a CPA and an estate attorney, why do I need to read the rest of this guide? Isn't it their job to know all this stuff?" The answer is yes—and no.

- **Ed Slott's advice:** Yes, your advisors should know all of the information in this guide. But as their employer, you need to be up on the best strategies for your needs and raise key issues with them. Smart retirement planning is an ongoing dialogue with advisors followed by action and fine-tuning along the way. The more you know, the better you'll be able to manage the process, protect your interests and prosper in retirement.

39. Big risks to your IRA savings

IRA planning is largely about maximizing the odds of reaching financial goals —and minimizing the risks that your wealth faces. These risks come in all shapes and sizes—including a recession, job loss, costly health crises, an unexpected death and even living longer than expected. Here's how these risks can be reduced:

- **Portfolio threats**—Market and economic risks to your IRA portfolio are offset through proper asset allocation, diversification and hedging.

- **Job threats**—The risk that IRA assets will be needed to pay bills following a layoff can be offset by setting aside enough emergency cash to cover your expenses until reemployment.

- **Health threats**—The risk that your IRA assets will be dramatically reduced to pay for health care is offset with health, disability and long-term care insurance.

- **Legacy threats**—The risk that your death will leave your family without sufficient income over time or that heirs won't inherit what you intended is offset with life insurance.

- **Tax threats**—The risk that your estate will owe more than necessary when you die in estate and income taxes is offset through strategic estate and tax planning.

40. Estate taxes made simple

When you die, the IRS considers all of the assets that are titled in your name or held jointly with your spouse to be part of your estate. The tax law generally allows you to pass all of your assets to your spouse tax-free. But if you die without a spouse, or you've left assets to children and other non-spouse heirs, these assets are tallied up and may face federal and state estate taxes. Such assets include the value of your retirement plans, your taxable accounts, real estate, and all other items of value owned by you.

- **Ed Slott's advice:** To preserve as much of the wealth you've built up as possible and to avoid overpaying your taxes, you and your financial advisor and estate attorney need to take steps to legally minimize the likelihood of taxation.

41. The case of the two Uncle Sams

When you die, your assets pass either to your spouse—or to children and other non-spouse heirs. Who gets what is spelled out in your will and in your retirement account beneficiary forms.

- **Problem:** Most estates will not pay federal estate tax, but some states have a state estate tax. The estate level at which state taxation begins is generally significantly lower. The federal government lets you subtract the amount of estate tax paid to a state from your federal estate-tax liability, up to a limit.

- **Ed Slott's advice:** Talk with your financial advisor and accountant about ways to minimize the impact of federal and state estate taxes. This is often done through gifting and life insurance, for example.

42. Avoid this death-benefit trap

When you take out a life insurance policy on your life, you typically name someone who will receive the cash death benefit when you die. This person is known as the policy's "beneficiary." If the beneficiary is your spouse, no estate taxes will generally be owed. But if the beneficiary is a child or other non-spouse heir, the death benefit will be counted as part of your estate and may be needed to pay estate taxes, reducing the cash payout.

- **Problem:** If you die and your spouse inherits your assets, no taxes are generally owed. But when your spouse dies, his or her much-larger estate will likely pass to your children, increasing the odds of an estate tax.

- **Ed Slott's advice:** While this is not a problem for most individuals in 2021 since the estate tax exemption is $11,700,000 per person (this amount sunsets after 2025) and is portable to a surviving spouse, ask your financial advisor and estate attorney about ways to minimize estate taxes when a surviving spouse dies.

43. What is term life insurance?

Term life insurance is the most basic type of policy. You pay a relatively low annual premium for coverage that remains in force for a specific number of years (the "term")—provided the premiums are paid. You can buy a "level term" policy in which the premium stays the same annually for the duration of the policy. Or you can buy annual renewable term, in which the premium starts out very low but inches up annually over the policy's term.

- **Ed Slott's advice:** A term policy typically is ideal for young couples who don't have a significant amount of income and want to maximize coverage and minimize annual premiums.

44. What is permanent life insurance?

The alternative to term life insurance is "permanent" insurance, which remains in force for the duration of your life, not a specific term—as long as the required annual premiums are paid. The premium for a permanent policy is higher than that for a term policy with the same death benefit for two reasons: The policy is in force for life, and part of your premium is deposited into a savings or "cash value" component. There are different kinds of permanent life insurance, so be sure to discuss them with your financial advisor or an insurance agent.

Retirement cash flow from life insurance

Most life insurance policies offer a prime tax benefit. When the insured individual dies, the beneficiary collects a death benefit and owes no income tax. That's true even if the decedent had paid, say, $500 in annual premiums and the beneficiary receives $250,000 or more from the insurer.

Some permanent life insurance policies have cash value. This generates two more tax benefits:

- **Tax-free buildup.** Cash value accumulation is not subject to income tax, inside the policy.

- **Tax-free lifetime cash flow.** The owner of a permanent life policy can withdraw money or take policy loans. This cash flow may be untaxed.

Generally, it takes years for such opportunities to become available. Permanent life policies often have upfront costs that depress the initial cash value. Eventually, sound policies can have substantial cash value, which the policyholder can tap.

Life insurance companies frequently provide "illustrations" to consumers considering permanent life insurance. These illustrations may show years of paying premiums followed by years of untaxed withdrawals or untaxed policy loans, or both. The illustrated cash flow to a living policy owner may be far greater than the premiums paid over time.

- **Ed Slott's advice:** You should buy life insurance because there is a genuine need for the death benefit, such as providing financial support to surviving loved ones. Once you decide to buy life insurance, and how much coverage you need, a permanent life policy might be a good choice if you are in it for the long term. After you have had a permanent life policy for a while and your cash value is substantial, you may decide to supplement your retirement income with periodic policy loans and withdrawals, tax-free. Just keep in mind that accessing your policy in that manner probably will reduce the death benefit.

  Warning! If you tap your policy for retirement cash flow, do so prudently. If you withdraw or borrow too heavily, your cash value may become insufficient and your policy might lapse. Not only would you lose your insurance coverage, you also could owe income tax on the investment earnings that had previously been sheltered inside the policy!

  Your insurance agent should be able to help you keep policy loans and withdrawals within acceptable levels.

45. How to protect your wealth

If the value of your estate is significant and will likely face estate taxes when you die ($11.7 million for individuals and $23.4 million for married couples in 2021), consider taking out a life insurance policy to cover the estate-tax tab. The death benefit of this policy will keep heirs from having to dip into the estate (their inheritance) to pay Uncle Sam.

46. Life insurance: Old and/or ill?

When it comes to buying life insurance, don't assume that someone who is old or ill won't qualify for a policy. If you want to cover sizable estate taxes with a life insurance policy, you almost always can secure coverage:

- **Little-known fact:** Some insurers have quotas to fill, and toward the end of each year will issue policies to even old and ill individuals by charging a high one-time premium.

47. Avoid this life insurance trap

To maximize the death benefit of a life insurance policy, don't own it in your name. If you own the policy in your name, the death benefit's value will be included as part of your estate and be subject to estate taxes, reducing the cash your non-spouse heirs will receive.

- **Ed Slott's advice:** Own the policy outside of your estate— perhaps by a trust. By having a trust own the policy, you're still insured and the death benefit will still be available to heirs. Upon your death, the policy's death benefit will pour into the trust— and not be included as part of your estate. Heirs will wind up receiving distributions from the trust based on the trust's terms.

48. Consider a life insurance trust

Many people who amass sizable estates by the time they retire wonder how they can pass as much of it as possible to heirs.

- **Tax traps:** You can't just hand the assets to heirs while you're alive. Uncle Sam can take an enormous bite in the form of a gift tax (visit **irahelp.com/2021** for the latest levels). On the other hand, if you wait until you die, the assets will be considered part of your estate and may face federal and state estate taxes.

- **Ed Slott's advice:** You can avoid any future estate tax traps by setting up a life insurance trust as the owner and beneficiary of a life insurance policy and naming heirs as the trust's beneficiaries. Then when you die, the sizable death benefit passes into the trust and is excluded from your estate. As a result, your heirs receive every dime you intended for them, not Uncle Sam. In addition, because of the changes made by the 2019 retirement plan law (the SECURE Act), setting up a life insurance trust may be a better idea than naming a trust as your IRA beneficiary.

49. Use your IRA to pay premiums

One way to pay a life insurance premium after age 59½ is to use your IRA. If you own a traditional IRA, you'll owe income tax on the amount withdrawn. But the move still may pay since you'll be providing heirs with a tax-free inheritance in the form of the insurance policy's death benefit.

- **Ed Slott's advice:** If you believe that the top tax rates are likely to rise substantially in the years ahead, then it's far more attractive to pay the lower income tax now. Of course, this strategy makes sense only if the funds in an IRA or savings account aren't needed to pay your bills. Also ask your estate attorney and accountant about setting up a life insurance trust.

50. Provide for heirs and spend freely

Many people sacrifice for their kids. But most people go too far, tightening the screws on savings and enjoyment to ensure that heirs wind up with the largest possible inheritance, which is certainly noble. But what if you could leave heirs exactly what you want them to receive—and still enjoy your savings?

- **Ed Slott's advice:** Take a portion of your savings and buy a life insurance policy with a death benefit that covers what you want heirs to have. By doing this, heirs are covered and you're able to spend your savings as you wish. Just be sure to do this as early in life as possible, before health issues emerge and push premium costs up. After the 2019 retirement plan law (the SECURE Act), buying life insurance may make more sense than leaving IRA assets to heirs.

51. What's an annuity?

An annuity is purchased through an insurance company and guarantees the owner payments over a set number of years—or until death. An annuity can be purchased with a guaranteed death benefit—which means if you die, your beneficiaries will receive at least what you paid in premiums.

52. What are the annuity types?

There are two basic types of annuities—immediate and deferred:

- **Immediate annuity**—you invest a lump sum, typically at retirement. Regular payments from the annuity start immediately. **Deferred annuity**—you invest and your contributions grow tax-deferred, like in a traditional IRA. You can choose between a fixed or variable deferred annuity, depending on your tolerance for risk. Fixed means your contributions go into investments that earn a fixed rate of interest. Variable means your contributions grow based on market conditions, since they are typically invested in stock and bond annuity funds.

53. Why is an annuity attractive?

An annuity is designed to produce income for its owner in retirement. As a result, an annuity can function like a pension, making regular monthly payments. Such payments keep you from worrying that declining financial markets or the economy will hurt your investment income stream.

- **Ed Slott's advice:** An annuity can be used as a hedge, providing you with a guaranteed income stream that your stock portfolio was supposed to generate but might not if the economy declines.

54. Why buy an annuity in an IRA?

Many advisors frown upon buying an annuity in an IRA, since annuity contributions already grow on a tax-deferred basis. But what if you don't have enough cash in a taxable account to buy an annuity that pays guaranteed income? That's when it may make sense to use IRA assets to buy an annuity within the IRA. Discuss your options with your financial advisor.

55. Aren't annuity fees high?

Admittedly, some annuities tend to have higher fees than other types of investments. But annuities can provide guaranteed income regardless of economic meltdowns and come with a death benefit, so they can't really be compared to most other investments.

- **Ed Slott's advice:** When comparing fees, weigh them against other annuities issued by insurance companies with similar attributes and ratings.

56. Essential estate-planning documents

Most Americans do not have a will or other estate documents. And if they do, the documents aren't likely up to date. What you need an estate attorney to draw up:

- **A will**—ensures that qualifying assets are distributed according to your wishes. It also names a guardian for minor children.

- **Durable power of attorney**—names a family member or friend to make financial decisions for you if you're incapacitated or unable to act.

- **Health-care proxy**—authorizes a family member or friend to make medical decisions if you are incapacitated. Make sure your doctor and hospital have an up-to-date copy.

- **Living will**—states your health-care and end-of-life wishes so the person making decisions knows what you want. Make sure your doctor and hospital also have this document.

- **Medical release**—Often called a HIPAA release (Health Insurance Portability and Accountability Act), this document lets a family member or friend access your medical records to monitor what is going on and make decisions.

Chapter 4:

IRA Strategies

57. Affluent? You still can own a Roth IRA

You may be interested in contributing to a Roth IRA but think your income is too high. Are you out of luck? The answer is "no" and tax reform makes this clearer than ever by allowing a back-door Roth IRA conversion.

In 2021, if your modified adjusted gross income exceeds $208,000 (couples filing jointly) or $140,000 (single taxpayers), the tax code prohibits you from contributing to a Roth IRA (visit **irahelp.com/2021** for all 2021 IRA and tax tables). If your income exceeds these limits, take the following steps to own a Roth IRA:

Step 1: Open a new 2021 traditional IRA if you don't already have one before April 15, 2022, if you otherwise qualify (see tip #6). Because of the SECURE Act change removing the age 70½ restriction on traditional IRA contributions, folks over 70½ can now take advantage of the back-door Roth IRA conversion.

Step 2: Make the maximum 2021 contribution—$6,000 if you're age 49 or younger, $7,000 if you're age 50 or older.

Step 3: Convert funds to a Roth IRA, which you've been allowed to do since the income limit restrictions were waived in 2010.

Step 4: Mind the rules. You'll owe income tax on the conversion if you convert pre-tax funds, and the pro-rata rule will apply if you have after-tax funds in any of your IRAs. You won't be allowed to contribute to your new Roth IRA if your income exceeds the annual IRS limits. Consult a financial advisor or accountant with specialized knowledge in this area.

Step 5: Exploit the loophole. Get around the income restriction by repeating this contribution-conversion strategy year after year.

- **In the past,** there have been concerns about the legality of back-door Roth IRA conversions. To some, this strategy seemed too good to be true and an attempt to exploit a loophole. These transactions have been consistently dogged by rumors that Congress or the IRS was ready to shut them down.

  Congress has put these fears to rest by confirming that the back-door Roth is an allowable strategy, with several references to the back-door Roth strategy included in Congress' Conference Committee report that accompanies the new law. IRS has also stated that this strategy is allowed.

58. Can Uncle Sam change his mind?

While you can convert a traditional IRA to a Roth IRA regardless of your income, many people worry that the deficit-weary federal government will change its mind about the tax-free withdrawal status of Roth IRAs.

- **Ed Slott's advice:** Congress did change its mind about the "stretch IRA" (see tip #109), so we can never be certain. However, besides the political risks of officials advocating for such a change, Roth IRAs are funded with after-tax dollars. If taxes were to be imposed on Roth IRAs, no one would fund them, boxing the government out of tax revenue. Even if the Roth IRA's tax-free status were to change, existing accounts would likely be exempt from the new rules.

59. IRA conversion? Watch your 401(k)

If you're planning to convert a traditional IRA to a Roth IRA, delay rolling over a 401(k) from a past employer into your traditional IRA until the year following the conversion.

- **Reason:** For tax purposes, you want to keep your percentage of nondeductible contributions higher in the pro-rata formula the IRS uses to determine taxation on a conversion.
- **Ed Slott's advice:** You'll need to know which of your past IRA contributions were deductible and nondeductible. Consult your financial planner and accountant before making a move.

60. IRA conversion? Mind your annuity

If you hold a variable annuity in a traditional IRA you plan to convert to a Roth IRA, have your financial advisor evaluate the annuity's value carefully. You can't use artificially deflated values for variable annuities.

- **Ed Slott's advice:** Get the actual fair-market value of the annuity from the issuing insurer.

61. Be sure of a Roth IRA conversion

The Tax Cuts and Jobs Act repealed the portion of the tax code that allowed for Roth recharacterizations. A recharacterization allowed a taxpayer to undo a Roth conversion as if it never happened. The benefits of a Roth IRA conversion remain unchanged — *you trade a tax bill now in exchange for tax-free Roth IRA distributions down the road.* That is still going to be a good deal for many people. Now that we are living in a world without recharacterization, you need to be very sure that it is the right strategy for you. With the "do-over" option no longer available, it is more important than ever that you work with an educated financial advisor and carefully consider all the pros and cons before doing a Roth IRA conversion.

Note that Congress kept the ability for taxpayers to recharacterize contributions. An IRA contribution can be recharacterized to a Roth IRA contribution and vice-versa. So be sure to consult with an educated financial advisor.

62. No life insurance? Convert an IRA

Does a health problem make it impossible for you to qualify for life insurance? Or is a policy's annual premium prohibitively expensive? If you want non-spouse heirs such as children to inherit a sizable sum when you die, consider converting your traditional IRA to a Roth IRA and naming those heirs as beneficiaries.

- **Reason:** During your life, there are no required distributions from your Roth IRA, and the Roth IRA will pass income-tax free to designated heirs provided five years have elapsed prior to inheritance.

- **Ed Slott's advice:** Be sure non-spouse heirs are named as beneficiaries on the newly converted Roth IRA.

63. When to decline an IRA inheritance

When one spouse dies, the surviving spouse is most often the beneficiary of the decedent's IRA. But the surviving spouse doesn't have to accept the inheritance. You have nine months to decline (disclaim) assets meant for you to inherit. Why would anyone decline to inherit an IRA? Here are the main reasons:

- **Assets aren't needed.** A surviving spouse with sufficient assets (or who receives life insurance proceeds) may not need the IRA assets and may want children or grandchildren to inherit them instead. By declining the inheritance, the IRA will pass to the next person named on the IRA's beneficiary form.

- **Estate-tax risk.** A surviving spouse inherits his or her spouse's assets tax-free. But when those assets pass to a spouse, they could result in a much larger estate when the surviving spouse dies, resulting in a stiff estate tax.

- **Ed Slott's advice:** One way to avoid passing along a future estate tax is to decline the IRA inheritance. When this happens, the assets will be counted as part of the decedent's estate and may face estate taxes. Then the heirs next in line as beneficiaries will receive the assets. Disclaiming an inheritance is tricky. Before accepting assets, talk to your financial advisor and accountant.

64. Tricky IRA inheritance issues

Leaving assets to your spouse or a single heir is easy. But what if your life is more complicated? Here are three common inheritance scenarios that you should discuss with your advisor and estate attorney:

- **Multiple heirs**—IRA owners who want to pass IRA assets to multiple non-spouse heirs often wonder how to divide the wealth. First, complete the IRA beneficiary form so that all heirs are named. As for the share, dividing the inheritance equally by percentage is often easier and less likely to produce feuds than trying to divide assets fairly by dollars based on heirs' means.

- **New spouse**—People who divorce and remarry need to revisit whom they want to inherit their IRA.

- **Single asset**—Naming IRA heirs is relatively simple. You complete the beneficiary form, and assets pass accordingly upon death. But if you are passing a home—an asset that can't neatly be divided—enormous friction can result if you leave heirs to figure out how to share the asset. Ask your estate attorney for strategies to ensure that the property passes equitably and that there are provisions in place for sharing or selling the property and protecting against possible taxes.

65. Steps if you inherit an IRA

The first step is to do nothing. You first want to hire a financial advisor who is educated in IRA strategies and distributions (see tips #29-34). Here are the issues you need to discuss with that advisor:

- **Accept or decline**—Just because you are the named beneficiary of an IRA doesn't mean you must accept it. In some cases, declining the inherited IRA may make more sense from a tax perspective.

- **Title properly**—If you accept the inherited IRA and you are not the spouse of the deceased, the IRA needs to be properly titled. It cannot be rolled into your existing IRA.

- **Distributions**—If you're not the spouse, you will probably have to receive the entire share of your inherited IRA within 10 years of the owner's death. However, if you are an "eligible designated beneficiary" (see tip #110), take minimum distributions each year based on the IRS' life-expectancy table. Minimum distributions by a non-spouse eligible designated beneficiary must begin by December 31 of the year following the year of the IRA owner's death.

- **Beneficiary**—You will need to name a beneficiary for your Inherited IRA in case something happens to you. This is done by filling out the inherited IRA's beneficiary form.

- **Ed Slott's advice:** Avoid the temptation to withdraw the entire lump sum you inherit. For one, you'll face income tax on the full amount distributed to you. For another, the longer you leave assets in an account that can grow tax-free, the more you're likely to have over time. This is true even if you must receive all of the inherited IRA assets within 10 years of the owner's death.

66. Do you qualify for an IRD deduction?

In the past, the IRD deduction was one of the most overlooked tax breaks available to inheritors of an IRA, 401(k) or other property. But now with the increased estate tax exemptions, it will only be used by those who inherit from very large estates.

- **How it works:** If you inherit an IRA and take distributions, you'll owe income tax on the amount withdrawn. But if the person you inherited from had an estate that paid federal estate taxes, you are entitled to the IRD deduction, which can range as high as 40%.

- **Ed Slott's advice:** The IRD deduction can save you significant taxes and also is exempt from the alternative minimum tax (AMT). But figuring out your tax savings can be tricky, so consult your financial advisor or accountant.

67. Update your plan as life changes

You now have plenty of actionable, useful information to create a proactive plan to keep more of the money you have earned and make it last as long as you do. But, any plan has to leave room for changes and revisions as new events in your life unfold.

For example, events such as a birth, an illness, a death, an inheritance, a marriage, a divorce, a remarriage, new grandchild, etc. You get the idea. As situations change in your life, use the information in this guide to adapt and revise your plans, maybe changing a beneficiary or altering your estate plan. Tax law changes, such as those made by the SECURE Act, also need to be considered since they can have a major impact, especially when it comes to your tax-deferred retirement savings.

- **Ed Slott's advice:** Anticipate change, and when it comes, embrace it and ACT. It is essential to make educated and informed decisions, but they need to be reviewed and often revised to reflect changes in your life or new tax laws. Your plan should always be based on the most current information available, including the important changes made by the SECURE Act.

Chapter 5:

In Retirement

68. Can you afford to retire?

As you near retirement, you and your financial advisor need to calculate whether your savings will be able to meet your annual needs, which debts need to be paid off, and which accounts you'll turn to first for your post-retirement needs.

- **Ed Slott's advice:** With your financial advisor, make a list of income sources, including IRAs and other savings accounts, Social Security, pensions, etc. Determine how these assets need to be invested to match your risk tolerance and to be preserved for life expectancy. Also, find out how much to withdraw from which accounts.

69. Will your savings last a lifetime?

When you're young, your big goal is to save enough for retirement. When you retire, your big goal is to make sure you don't run out of what you've saved. Most people live longer than they assumed they would.

- **Ed Slott's advice:** Before you retire, consider whether you have enough to sustain your lifestyle during your retirement years. Then take steps to protect against devastating risks to those assets. Talk to your financial advisor about buying annuities to produce steady income for life. You can reduce the cost by buying annuities that don't start making payments until age 85, for example. Also discuss the savings realized if you move to a smaller home and take out long-term care insurance to minimize risks to savings.

70. Pre-retirement advisor questions

1. **How** much will I need to live on each year?
2. **What** sources will fund this amount?
3. **Which** assets should I turn to first if I'm at least age 59½?
4. **How** can I increase investment income?
5. **How** much emergency cash should I set aside?
6. **What** debts should I pay off before retirement?
7. **Should** I roll my 401(k) into my IRA?
8. **Should** I convert all or part of my traditional IRA into a Roth IRA?
9. **How** can I make sure my life insurance policy is on schedule to pay off?
10. **Do** I need long-term care insurance?

71. Watch those nest-egg raids

Retirees who fear running out of assets in retirement frequently wonder how much they can safely withdraw from savings annually to fund their lifestyle.

- **Ed Slott's advice:** A withdrawal rate of 4% per year is a good starting point when considering how to draw down your assets without running out of money. Withdrawal rates above 4% will increase the odds of running out of cash. Discuss this with your financial advisor so that all of your income assets are considered and factored into the withdrawal equation.

Playing by the "4% Rule"

The good news is that you probably won't run out of money in retirement, as long as the federal government can transfer electronic Social Security payments into your bank account. The bad news? You may well run short of cash if you live beyond your life expectancy and deplete your portfolio.

To address this concern, financial advisors and academic researchers have come up with what's known as the 4% Rule. Here's the premise:

- **In the first year of your retirement** you should draw down no more than 4% of your portfolio.

- **In each succeeding year,** you can increase your portfolio withdrawal to keep up with inflation.

- **Judging by historic market returns,** this strategy will provide a high probability that your portfolio will last for 30 years or longer.

To put some numbers to this plan, assume that Fran retires with a $600,000 portfolio. In her first year without receiving a paycheck, she withdraws $24,000 (4% of $600,000) from her portfolio for spending money.

Assume that inflation is 3% that year. In Year Two of her retirement, Fran adds 3% ($720) to her annual drawdown, pulling out $24,720.

Suppose that inflation the next year goes up to 5%, so Fran would be scheduled to withdraw 5% more in Year Three, or $25,956. She could round up to a $26,000, to keep things simple.

And so on, year after year. Fran eventually will be withdrawing $30,000 or $40,000 or more in a given year with this plan, depending on how long she lives and the rate of inflation. Nevertheless, it's very likely her portfolio will last as long as she does.

- **Judgment calls.** Keep in mind that there is no penalty for bending the rules. You might, for example, skip the annual inflation increase after a steep drop in portfolio value. Alternatively, you might start with, say, a 5% withdrawal instead of 4% if you plan to eventually sell a valuable home and move into less expensive housing.

  In any case, you should realize that even a 4% withdrawal rate is greater than the current yields from stock dividends and high-quality bond interest. To draw down your portfolio in line with the 4% rule, you probably will have to sell some assets. Ask your wealth advisor to help you develop a plan for liquidating your portfolio assets.

- **Ed Slott's advice:** The main takeaway here is to make sure you have an idea about what size retirement fund you'll need to support your lifestyle. If you would like to withdraw $40,000 a year in your retirement, adjusted for inflation, you'd need a $1 million portfolio, using the 4% Rule. Increased saving may be the only way you can accumulate the desired amount by your retirement target date. Similarly, if you are already in retirement, the 4% rule can help you determine whether or not you may need to adjust your lifestyle in order to avoid running out of money.

72. When to take Social Security

Consider waiting until age 70 to receive Social Security checks. Your monthly payments will be higher than if you began at age 62 or 66, and over a long life the total payout will also be higher. But it is a complex decision, involving other assets, income taxes and estate plans, so it is best discussed with a financial advisor.

73. How to trim wasteful spending

Budgeting is hard for most people—particularly if you don't have a head for numbers or aren't highly organized. Spending is easy when you're younger and employed, because you have income coming in each month. But in retirement, watching where your dollars go is essential. The goal is to make your savings last.

- **Ed Slott's advice:** Make a list of your three types of monthly expenses —fixed costs such as utilities; flexible expenses such as food and gasoline; and discretionary expenses such as entertainment and travel. Get your monthly bills and jot down what you paid. Then add up the monthly total and multiply it by 12 for your estimated annual expenses. Don't forget to include insurance premiums, taxes and any other periodic expenses. Look for ways to reduce costs by saving money on flexible expenses and cutting back on discretionary expenses.

74. Keep savings safe and sound

We know that anything can happen to the economy—and at any time. The key, clearly, is not to be exposed to excessive risk when you need to preserve your retirement savings.

- **Ed Slott's advice:** Make sure your IRA and other savings accounts are properly allocated for your age and tolerance for risk. In retirement, your biggest risk is defined as running out of money.

75. When to take IRA withdrawals

If you're a retiree who's at least age 59½ and unsure whether to withdraw assets from your IRA, talk first with your financial advisor and accountant. Ideally, you want to take withdrawals from taxable accounts first before turning to an IRA. That's because the longer you leave assets in an IRA, the longer they can compound tax-free.

- **Ed Slott's advice:** When you withdraw assets from a traditional IRA, calculate your tax hit immediately and set aside the cash. Too many people withdraw assets and spend it all. Then when tax time arrives, they don't have the money to pay Uncle Sam.

Avoid early withdrawal penalties

Your IRA is meant to provide retirement income, so there is generally a 10% early withdrawal penalty before you reach age 59½. That penalty is added to your regular income tax.

Suppose that Greg, age 52, pulls $10,000 from his IRA. If he is in a 22% tax bracket, he will owe $2,200 (22% of $10,000) in tax. He'll also owe a $1,000 penalty (10% of $10,000), so his effective tax rate on early withdrawals will be 32%.

- **Out of the penalty box.** Fortunately, there are several exceptions to the early withdrawal penalty. If Greg qualifies, he'll owe the $2,200 regular tax but not the $1,000 penalty.

Among several exceptions to the penalty, consider these:

- **Deductible medical expenses.** Suppose that Greg's adjusted gross income (AGI) is $60,000 this year and his unreimbursed medical expenses are $7,500. Greg will generally be entitled to deduct medical costs over 7.5% of his AGI: $7,500- $4,500 = $3,000. Thus, $3,000 of Greg's $10,000 IRA withdrawal will escape the 10% penalty. This exception applies even if Greg does not itemize deductions on this year's tax return.

- **Health insurance.** Say Greg has lost his job this year and collected unemployment for at least 12 consecutive weeks. He paid a total of $4,800 for family coverage during the year. Greg can withdraw up to $4,800 from his IRA, penalty free.

- **College bills.** In another scenario, Greg pays $5,000 towards his son's college education this year as well as $2,000 so he can take a night school course towards his MBA. If so, he can take up to $7,000 from his IRA this year without owing the 10% penalty.

- **First home.** Greg also can take up to $10,000 from his IRA, penalty-free, to help pay for a first-time home purchase. The money might be used to help Greg's daughter buy her first home or for a home purchase by Greg himself, after going more than two years without owning a home. Note the last part of that sentence. "First-time homebuyer" doesn't have to mean first home, but the $10,000 number is a lifetime cap, not one you can utilize in totality for another home purchase five years down the road.

- **Disability.** If Greg becomes disabled and can't work, IRA distributions escape the 10% penalty.

- **Annuity.** Regardless of whether you are buying a first home or paying college bills or otherwise qualify for an exception, you can avoid the 10% early withdrawal penalty by taking a series of substantially equal periodic payments (SOSEPPs) from your IRA over your life expectancy.

- **Ed Slott's advice:** The SOSEPP rules are included in Section 72(t) of the tax code. By going to an Internet search engine, you can find many 72(t) calculators.

Suppose that Greg goes to an Internet 72(t) calculator and finds an approved method that permits him to withdraw $9,953 a year, penalty-free, from his $300,000 IRA. Greg takes that amount from his IRA and begins a SOSEPP.

A SOSEPP for this purpose must last five years or until age 59½, whichever comes later. Thus, Greg—now age 52—must take exactly $9,953 from his IRA each year until he reaches 59½. Any departure from this path will result in the 10% penalty being imposed on all of Greg's pre-59½ IRA withdrawals, plus interest. Work with your IRA custodian to set up your SOSEPP withdrawals.

- **Birth or adoption.** The SECURE Act added an exception for penalty-free IRA withdrawals after birth or adoption. The withdrawal must take place within one year from the birth date or when the adoption is finalized. Adopted children must be under age 18 or disabled under the Tax Code's strict definition. There is a $5,000 limit (per parent) on withdrawals for each birth or adoption. Withdrawn amounts can be repaid to the IRA at any future time.

76. Retiree tax breaks in 2021

Retirees get breaks on airlines and movie tickets. They also get breaks from the tax code:

- **Capital gains.** If you're in the lower tax brackets, long-term capital gains in 2021 are not taxed.

  As always, go to my website **irahelp.com** to find out the latest on this and any other major tax rule changes that could affect your retirement savings.

- **Real estate sales.** If you want to sell your home to relocate to a smaller one and you've owned your home for 20 or 30 years, your gain on the sale may exceed the tax exclusions of $500,000 for a couple or $250,000 for a single filer. To avoid capital gains taxes, you need to have big carry-forward losses from last year or sell portfolio losers to offset the gains on the home sale.

- **Reduce your estate.** If you have sizable assets that comfortably exceed what you'll need in retirement, consider making gifts to reduce your taxable estates (visit **irahelp.com/2021** for the latest maximum levels). You also can pay education expenses for grandchildren gift-tax free, provided your check is made out to the school. Or you can contribute to a 529 Education Savings

Plan. Beginning in 2018, 529 accounts can be used to pay for K-12 education expenses.

77. Convert an IRA in retirement?

Much depends on your tax bracket in retirement and whether you have cash on hand to pay the income-tax bill. Starting in 2010, the IRS allowed all taxpayers to convert part or all of a traditional IRA, a 401(k) or other company plan to a tax-free Roth IRA—regardless of household income! The catch? You have to pay income tax on the fair-market value of the account at the time of conversion. Which means you need the cash to do this.

- **Ed Slott's advice:** Many retirees live longer than expected, making a partial or full conversion extremely tax efficient. That's because the account is likely to grow over time and then pass to heirs tax-free—provided you have had a Roth IRA for five years. Also likely: Your current tax bracket may be higher in the future.

78. Convert an IRA for inheritance?

If you plan to pass your IRA to your children, converting part or all of your traditional IRA to a Roth IRA likely makes sense. By converting, you will not have to take mandatory distributions starting at age 72. Also, your children will not owe federal income tax on the Roth IRA they inherit provided you have had a Roth IRA for five years. If you're over age 59½, you can use the traditional IRA assets to pay the tax without facing an early-withdrawal penalty. Better yet, pay the tax with other assets.

- **Ed Slott's advice:** If your goal is to pass any IRA to your children, be sure they are named on the IRA's beneficiary form.

79. Beware this IRA conversion trap

If you're already taking required minimum distributions (RMDs) from a traditional IRA, you cannot dodge the annual RMD by converting the IRA to a Roth IRA. Rule: You must first take the required minimum distribution for the year and then convert the remaining traditional IRA to a Roth IRA.

80. Know the IRA withdrawal rules

Starting at age 72, you are required to begin taking distributions from a traditional IRA. But how much do you have to take? That depends how you stack up on the IRS' life-expectancy tables. Each year's required minimum distribution is determined by dividing your IRA balance by the number of years the IRS expects you to be around.

- **Doing the math:** Check the IRS life-expectancy table at **irahelp.com/2021.** To calculate your 2021 RMD, find your age. Then divide the value of your IRA at the end of last year by the corresponding "distribution period." Or ask your accountant.

81. Watch out for retiree scams

Retirees are prime candidates for a wide range of financial scams and schemes. Beware of the following:

- **New advisors**—Always vet a new financial advisor, CPA or lawyer with care by running a background check on their credentials, education and any liens and legal actions pending.

- **Hot tips**—It's very easy to fall prey to advice from friends who claim to have done well with a particular investment. Resist the temptation to get in on the action. In most cases, such ventures may not be right for you and could wind up in disaster.

- **Phone pitches**—Don't be suckered by phone calls from people claiming to represent organizations and asking for personal information. The simple solution is to just hang up.

- **Door sales**—Steer clear of people who show up unannounced with low-cost offers to fix something on your house they've spotted from the street.

- **Social calls**—Beware of pitches from people who use the environment, animals, diseases or other heart-tuggers to hold your attention. Before donating to any charity, check on the charity's existence and make the donation directly through instructions on its website.

- **Pal of a pal**—Watch out for pitches by strangers who claim to be friends of your friends. This is one of the most effective ways to get victims to let down their guard.

- **Fishy e-mails**—Beware of e-mails from banks and financial institutions claiming there's a problem with your account. A real institution would not ask for personal information. To verify your account, never click on the link provided. Always go to your institution's website and access your account that way. Or call the number provided by the institution.

- **Going fast**—Avoid financial pitches that stress there's little time left, or there are only a few opportunities left for those who invest immediately.

- **New friends**—Sophisticated scammers befriend people and spend time developing trusting relationships before pitching a fraudulent deal.

- **Snail Mail**— IRS will always contact you by mail. Beware of e-mails or phone calls that say they are from the IRS, especially if they make threats.

82. Run a feud-free family meeting

Unless there's a reason why your children should not know about your finances, a family meeting with your financial advisor is a wise move—especially in retirement.

- **Ed Slott's advice:** Having your financial advisor present and officiating the meeting will keep the summit from sliding into personal issues or being used to settle old scores. By including your advisor, your children will receive a financial education, letting them become more confident managers of their finances and the advisors who are working for you.

83. Secrets of healthy family meetings

When you hold a family meeting with your financial advisor, draft questions and concerns in advance. Your children should know how to contact your life insurance representative, financial planners, accountants, and attorneys. In the meeting, note how the advisors respond to your children. This is a good indicator as to how helpful these advisors will be to your children in the future.

Chapter 6:
Social Security And Medicare*

A special thank you to Heather Schreiber, RICP®, founder of HLS Retirement Consulting, for her extensive contributions to this chapter on Social Security and Medicare. Heather is an expert in Social Security planning and retirement income strategies and, like Ed Slott, has a passion for consumer advocacy. For more information about Heather, visit hlsretirementconsulting.com.

84. What Uncle Sam has to offer

Don't neglect Social Security and Medicare in your retirement planning. The former is a pension from the federal government. You've paid for it throughout your working years so you can collect in retirement. In general, married couples can get two Social Security checks each month. Some exceptions apply, for example, if one or both worked for a federal, state, or local agency and received a pension based on non-covered earnings (i.e. not subject to social security taxes) or worked in another country.

Medicare is health insurance for seniors, generally age 65 or older. Medicare Part A (hospital insurance) is premium free, at age 65, if you or your spouse worked and paid Medicare taxes for at least 10 years. Part B (medical insurance) is available to most at a monthly premium of $148.50 for 2021.

- **Ed Slott's advice:** It's true that both Social Security and Medicare are currently expected to run short of money over the long run. However, tens of millions of American seniors are covered by these programs. Politicians in Washington will continue to tinker with their frameworks, but it's doubtful that benefits will be cut sharply. You can count on some form of Social Security and Medicare to be around when you retire.

Know Your Full Retirement Age (FRA)

When it comes to planning for Social Security benefits, there's one factor that's more important than just about everything else: your full retirement age (FRA). Many of the benefits you may be eligible for are calculated based on how long before or after your FRA you choose to collect them. Plus, if you were born on or before January 1, 1954, there may be a strategy that you can employ to enhance your lifetime benefits not necessary to say this part anymore since all eligible individuals are already past FRA as of January 1st 2020 (more on that later).

Your FRA has nothing to do with when you actually retire, but rather, it is determined solely by when you were born. So whether you retire at 50 (lucky you!) or you work until 85 (good for you!), your full retirement age is unaffected. Depending upon the year of your birth, your full retirement age may be anywhere from 65 – 67 (although if your FRA is under 66 you should already be claiming any Social Security benefits you're entitled to).

Use this chart to determine your FRA:

Full Retirement Age (FRA)

Year of Birth*	Full Retirement Age
1937 or earlier	65
1938	65 and 2 months
1939	65 and 4 months
1940	65 and 6 months
1941	65 and 8 months
1942	65 and 10 months
1943 - 1954	66
1955	66 and 2 months
1956	66 and 4 months
1957	66 and 6 months
1958	66 and 8 months
1959	66 and 10 months
1960 and later	67

*If you were born on January 1 of any year, you should refer to the previous year. If you were born on the 1st of the month, your benefit—and your full retirement age—is figured as if your birthday was in the previous month.

85. Working and Social Security may not mix

You can start collecting Social Security retirement benefits as early as age 62, but your benefit will be reduced for starting before your full retirement age. This reduction in your benefit is generally a permanent one. However, if you decide to file for benefits prior to your FRA while you are still working, you may also experience a reduction in your benefit due to the earnings limitation.

For example, suppose you receive benefits during a year you are younger than your full retirement age for the entire year and you expect to earn more than $18,960 in 2021, then you'll have $1 of Social Security benefits deducted for every $2 of income you earn over the limit. If you receive benefits during the year you reach full retirement age and earn more than $50,520 in 2021, then you'll have $1 of Social Security benefits deducted for every $3 of income you earn over the limit. This only applies to income you earn up to the month before your full retirement age. Any benefits previously withheld due to excess income will be paid back to you later in the form of a higher monthly benefit at your full retirement age.

- **Ed Slott's advice:** If you're still working before your full retirement age, it usually doesn't pay to start Social Security. What's more, the younger you are when you start to take benefits, the smaller your Social Security checks will be going forward. Married individuals who start before their full retirement age may lose the chance to maximize a couple's combined income from Social Security.

86. When sooner beats later

If you have stopped working, should you start Social Security at age 62, or soon thereafter? Maybe. It might make sense for one or both of these reasons.

- **You need the money.** With little or no earned income and a shortage of other resources, you might have to start Social Security for cash to pay your bills.

- **Your health isn't great.** By age 62, you might have developed a serious medical condition. Taking the money as soon as possible can make sense, especially if you are single. But, if you are married, be careful because your decision to file early could impact the survivor benefits for your spouse, particularly if you are the higher wage earner.

If you don't have an immediate need for the money and you're healthy enough to anticipate a long retirement, waiting will increase the size of the Social Security checks you'll eventually receive. Long-term, you may come out ahead.

87. Social Security's 8% solution

If you don't start Social Security at age 62, you can start any time after that. The waiting game ends at age 70, though. There's no point in waiting longer because your Social Security benefits won't increase any more moving forward.

- **Why you should wait.** If you collect at your full retirement age, you can expect to receive 100% of your benefit. On the other hand, if you choose to claim before your full retirement age, your benefit is reduced based on the number of months prior to your FRA you file; this could amount to as much as a 30% reduction. However, if you wait even a month or two after your full retirement age before claiming your benefit, you will receive a delayed retirement credit for each month that you wait to claim. This adds up to 8% in a 12-month period. That's 8% per year, guaranteed by the federal government, with no investment risk. Compare that with what you're getting now from your bank or your money market fund.

  What's more, that's 8% a year plus any cost-of-living boost. If inflation is, say, 3%, your total annual increase for waiting would be 11% that year.

  To give you an idea of the difference, suppose Al retires at his full retirement age (66) in 2021. Assuming Al had paid the maximum in Social Security taxes over his career, his monthly Social Security benefit would have been $3,113 which is the max benefit at FRA for 2021 or $37,356 a year. But if you make the same assumption about Carol, who retired at age 70 in 2021, her monthly benefit would have been $3,895 a month, or $46,740 per year – and that's not even counting any cost-of-living adjustments!

88. Waiting = longevity insurance

Some people approach the start-versus-wait decision by looking at the break-even calculation. You might say, how long will I have to live for the amounts added to my monthly checks to catch up with the money I didn't receive while I waited? That's one way to make the decision.

But don't forget to consider your spouse, particularly if you are the higher earning spouse.

Another way is to look at waiting as a means of buying "longevity insurance"—protection against running short of money in very old age. Today, many people are living into their late 80s, their 90s, and even hitting triple figures. That means 25+ years of retirement in many cases, and a real risk of emptying an investment portfolio. At that point, you'll really appreciate receiving a plumper Social Security check.

- **Ed Slott's advice:** The higher-earning spouse should generally wait to receive Social Security if that's practical. When one spouse dies, the survivor will continue to receive the larger of the two spouses' Social Security checks.

Coordinate with your spouse

If you are married, coordinating your own Social Security benefits with those of your spouse is an essential part of making sure you're maximizing the value of the Social Security benefits to which you're entitled. By coordinating your Social Security benefits with your spouse's benefits, you can help maximize income during both of your lifetimes, as well as for the survivor after one of you passes away. For a long time, the file-and suspend and restricted application strategies were two of the most common used by spouses to maximize Social Security benefits. Congress, however, passed a law in late 2015 eliminating these as potential strategies for many Boomers.

- **File and suspend –** Allows you to file for your Social Security benefits, but delay actually receiving those benefits. By doing so, your spouse may be able to claim a spousal benefit on your earnings history (which can only be done if you've filed). However, since you tell the Social Security Administration not to send you your own Social Security benefits, it allows them to continue to earn delayed credits.

  Warning! – You can only file and suspend once you've reached full retirement age or later. Additionally, suspending your benefit is no longer permitted for purposes of allowing a spouse to claim benefits while you suspended unless you affirmatively elected to suspend your benefits no later than April 29, 2016. As a result of the law Congress passed in late 2015, after that time, your spouse will only be able to collect a spousal benefit if you are receiving your own benefit.

File a restricted application – If your spouse has already filed for their own Social Security benefit or plans to do so, you may be able to file what's known as a "restricted application" to tell the Social Security Administration to pay you only your spousal benefit. Your own benefit will be unaffected and can continue to earn delayed credits.

Warning! – You can only file a restricted application once you've reached full retirement age or later, and you have not already filed for your own retirement benefit. In addition, this is only available to individuals who were age 66 or older by January 1, 2020. If you were born after January 1, 1954 and you file for your spousal benefit, you will also be deemed to be filing for your own benefit. This means that you will only be able to collect a spousal benefit if it is greater than your own.

89. IRAs can play a role in your Social Security decision

As you can see, waiting to start Social Security as late as possible, up to age 70, may pay off. But what if you need more cash flow while you're in your 60s? One approach is to tap your IRA then.

- **Conventional wisdom:** Many financial and tax advisors advocate delaying IRA distributions as long as possible. Required minimum distributions (RMDs) don't start until age 72 (unless you were 70½ or older by 12/31/19). The longer you continue tax-deferred buildup inside an IRA, the more wealth you can accumulate.

- **Ed Slott's unconventional advice:** Tapping your IRA during your 60s may be worthwhile if this tactic allows you to defer Social Security. Tax deferral inside an IRA is a real benefit, but this benefit is most valuable when you're in a high tax bracket and owe a substantial amount of income tax.

If you're in your 60s, in need of more cash flow, chances are that you have modest income and a small tax bill. Thus, IRA distributions won't be extremely taxing. Of course, once you're in your 60s, you're beyond the 10% early distribution penalty, which applies to those under age 59½.

90. A savvy sequence can slash your 70-something taxes

If you follow the traditional approach (start Social Security in your 60s, begin IRA withdrawals in your 70s), you probably will increase the income tax on your Social Security benefits. Reversing the procedure—drawing down your IRA so Social Security is delayed—can be a tax-saver.

Why? A full explanation would involve delving into one of the most arcane provisions of the tax code, which is saying a lot. Here's the simple version:

- **When you collect Social Security,** some or most of your benefits may be taxed.

- **This tax is determined by a formula.** The formula counts almost all of your income, including IRA withdrawals, but only half of your Social Security benefits.

- **By delaying Social Security,** you'll get a larger check each month. The larger your monthly check of half-counted benefits, the less you'll have to tap your fully-counted IRA for spending money.

- **Doing the math,** accelerating fully countable IRA dollars while delaying half-countable Social Security dollars can mean a smaller tax bill once you start collecting your heftier Social Security checks.

91. Crowding out the tax collector

Under current law, IRA distributions are fully taxed. If you withdraw $10,000 from your IRA, you add $10,000 to your taxable income for the year.

On the other hand, no more than 85% of your Social Security benefits are taxed under current law. If you receive $10,000 from Social Security, no more than $8,500 will be added to your taxable income for the year. Many seniors include less than 85% of their benefits in taxable income because they have moderate income, and some report no taxable benefits at all.

- **Ed Slott's advice:** Any strategy that substitutes Social Security benefits for IRA withdrawals will be a tax-saver. If overall income tax rates rise in the future, as many people expect, this form of retirement income arbitrage will become even more tax-efficient.

92. Make a good idea even better with Roth accounts

As already mentioned, while $1 of IRA withdrawals counts as $1 for determining the taxation of your Social Security benefits, $1 of Social Security benefits only counts as 50 cents. So it pays to load up on Social Security income and reduce taxable IRA distributions.

What's more, withdrawals from Roth IRAs and Roth 401(k)s are best of all: qualified Roth distributions aren't taxable income and they don't count at all on the formula for taxing your Social Security checks.

Say Carl and Donna have $50,000 of Roth IRA distributions a year plus $40,000 from Social Security benefits and no other income. This couple, with no other income, would owe no tax on their Social Security benefits under the formula. Roth IRA distributions are tax-free for taxpayers who are at least age 59½ and have held the accounts at least five years.

- **Ed Slott's advice:** Contributing to a Roth 401(k) is one way to get money into tax-free territory while you work. Once you retire, and your tax bracket drops, you can take money from taxable investment accounts to pay the tax on converting traditional IRA dollars to Roth IRA dollars.

93. Four for the money

Once you stop working, chances are you'll have four possible sources of income.

- **Taxable accounts.** This is money you have in banks, at brokers, or directly in mutual funds. These accounts have a variety of tax treatments. You may receive investment interest and dividends for spending money; you also can sell assets or take withdrawals to raise cash.

- **Tax-deferred accounts.** These include traditional IRAs, SEP IRAs, and SIMPLE IRAs. You also may have money you kept in an employer plan such as a 401(k) or a pension. For these accounts, withdrawals typically are fully or mostly taxable.

- **Tax-free accounts.** Roth IRAs and Roth-type employer plans such as Roth 401(k)s offer tax-free withdrawals. Typically, distributions are completely tax-free after five years and after age 59½.

- **Social Security.** This is a federal life-long pension for workers and their spouses. Depending on the amount and type of your other income, Social Security benefits are tax-free or partially taxable.

- **Ed Slott's advice:** You'll have more spendable income in retirement if you plan to coordinate these sources of future income. The younger you are when you start to plan, the more cash flow you're likely to enjoy.

94. Ed Slott's retirement income plan

After you stop working, you'll need cash for living expenses. Here's a simplified suggested sequence. In realty, some combination of withdrawals across different types of accounts often produces the most tax-efficient results:

1. **Start with your taxable accounts.** In these low-yield times, investment interest and dividends alone probably won't pay your bills. You'll need to take withdrawals and sell assets. Fortunately, taxes on these transactions are likely to be scant.

2. **Move money from tax-deferred accounts such as traditional IRAs and 401(k)s to your Roth IRA.** Again, these will be taxable transactions, but you probably won't owe much in tax if you're not working or you are in a lower tax bracket. Pay any tax from your taxable accounts.

3. **Draw down your tax-deferred accounts** once you've depleted your taxable accounts. Either use the money for spending or move dollars into your Roth IRA.

4. **Try to wait until age 70 to start Social Security benefits.**
    Among married couples, it sometimes makes sense for one
    spouse to start at full retirement age (66-67) while the other
    delays until 70. Dual-earner married couples who are 66 or
    older have the option to have the lower earning spouse file
    for benefits so that the higher earning spouse (who is at least
    age 66 by January 1, 2020) can file a restricted application
    before later switching over to his or her maximum benefit as
    late as age 70. Note that this doesn't require the lower earning
    spouse to also be 66; he or she only needs to be eligible to
    file for benefits so that the restricted filer can collect a spousal
    benefit. However, people who turned 66 on January 2, 2020
    or later are no longer able to claim a spousal benefit first and
    then later switch to a retirement benefit. Married retirees
    will now automatically receive the higher of the two benefit
    options and can no longer claim both types of payments at
    different times.

- **Bottom line:** The ideal endgame is to go into your 70s with
  maximum Social Security benefits and all of your savings in Roth
  accounts. Your Social Security benefits will be untaxed or lightly
  taxed, under current law, and qualified Roth distributions won't be
  taxed. Roth IRAs have no RMDs so money you don't need can pass
  to your beneficiaries, tax-free.

95. Learn the A-B-C-Ds of Medicare

Generally, Medicare is a great cost-saver. Workers and spouses typically
qualify at age 65. Assuming you're not covered by an employer's health
plan or by a former employer's retiree health benefits, you should sign
up because Medicare offers cost-effective health insurance. If you are
covered by another employer or retiree plan, it is always a good idea
to check with the employer to ensure that you shouldn't also sign up
for Medicare to avoid a late enrollment penalty. There are two main
components:

- **Part A.** This covers hospital bills after you pay a deductible of
  around $1,484 in 2021. For most seniors, there is no monthly
  charge for Part A.

- **Part B.** This covers doctors' visits and other medical expenses such as lab tests. The Standard Part B Premium is $148.50 in 2021.

- **Ed Slott's advice:** Don't think that Medicare covers all medical costs: it doesn't. You'll still have various out-of-pocket expenses for your health care, and they can be meaningful. Many people buy supplemental "Medigap" policies from private insurers to limit their exposure to medical bills and "Part D" policies to help pay for prescription drugs.

Alternatively, you can join "Medicare Part C," also known as Medicare Advantage, and sign up for comprehensive health coverage through a private company. You won't need a Medigap policy then and you probably won't need a Part D plan, either. Out-of-pocket costs will be limited. The catch, though, is that you'll have to go to certain doctors and hospitals to get the cost savings.

The Medicare website, **medicare.gov,** has a find-a-plan feature to help you decide if you want a Medicare Advantage plan and, if so, which one.

96. Beware of Medicare Part B Premiums

As mentioned, most Medicare enrollees pay about $148.50 per month for Part B medical coverage in 2021. Seniors with higher incomes pay more. The amount depends on your modified adjusted gross income (MAGI). For this purpose, your MAGI is your regular adjusted gross income, plus any (supposedly) tax-exempt interest from municipal bonds or bond funds. Generally speaking, Medicare Part B premiums are based off of your tax return from two years prior. So, for instance, your 2021 Medicare Part B premiums will generally be based on your 2019 income.

ED SLOTT'S
ELITE
IRA
ADVISOR GROUP
Find an advisor
at **irahelp.com**

In 2021, the standard Part B premium is $148.50 (or higher).

Here are the MAGI numbers for 2019 (for your 2021 premiums).

File individual tax return	File joint tax return	File married & Separate tax return	Monthly premium
$88,000 or less	$176,000 or less	$88,000 or less	$148.50
Above $88,000 up to $111,000	Above $176,000 up to $222,000	N/A	$207.90
Above $111,000 up tp $138,000	Above $222,000 up to $276,000	N/A	$297.00
Above $138,000 up to $165,000	Above $276,000 up to $330,000	N/A	$386.10
Up to $500,000	Up to $750,000	Up to $412,000	$475.20
Above $500,000	Above $750,000	Above $412,000	$504.90

Source: medicare.gov

Those Part B premium numbers are per Medicare enrollee. Thus, if a married couple includes two seniors on Medicare, with MAGI over $330,000, but less than $750,000, each spouse would owe $475.20 per month for Medicare Part B. That would be a total of $950.40 per month or more than $11,404 per year for health insurance.

97. Paring Part B premiums

Some planning can hold down your Medicare Part B premiums. The key is to realize that there is a two-year gap between actually receiving that high income and paying the super-premium for medical insurance. Consequently, since you may be eligible for Medicare at age 65, your reported income for every year starting at age 63 may determine your Part B premium. The earlier you start to plan, the better.

- **Ed Slott's advice:** A series of Roth IRA conversions can help you control your Part B premium. Any Roth IRA conversion after 2017 is irrevocable.

98. Appealing excessive Medicare premiums

As you can see, there's a time lag in imposing higher Part B premiums. What if you were working at age 63 or 64, earning a substantial amount, but retired by 65 or 66, with a much lower income? Can you ask for relief from the steep premium payments?

Yes, in some cases. If your income has gone down due to certain specific situations, you can ask for a lower premium. Those situations include:

1. You married, divorced, or became widowed.

2. You or your spouse stopped working or reduced your work hours.

3. You or your spouse lost income-producing property due to a disaster or other event beyond your control.

To support your claim, be ready to produce documentation, such as a death certificate or a letter from your former employer about your retirement.

99. Don't ignore the "health care IRA"

Before you reach Medicare age, you may be able to open a Health Savings Account (HSA). If so, an HSA can provide exceptional retirement planning opportunities, acting as an IRA for health care. HSAs can be extremely beneficial because they offer triple tax savings:

- **Tax-deductible contributions.**
- **Tax-free buildup** inside the HSA.
- **Tax-free distributions** for qualified health care expenses.

In order to have an HSA, you must have a qualified health insurance policy. Such policies have high deductibles, so you'll have low insurance premiums but ample out-of-pocket exposure before the insurance kicks in. With acceptable health insurance, you can contribute to an HSA—depending on your age and the coverage you have, deductible contributions could reach $8,200 in 2021 ($7,200 for family plus $1,000 catch up for those age 55 or over).

If you wish, you can tap your HSA to pay medical costs right away. There are no time limits on withdrawals, though, so you can keep your HSA intact, growing untaxed, and use it for a tax-free source of cash to pay medical bills in retirement, including prescription drugs and qualified long-term care services.

- **Ed Slott's advice:** Some observers believe that HSA contributions should be Step Two in your retirement planning each year, right after making 401(k) contributions that your employer will match. The triple tax benefits of HSAs are cited to support such assertions. That strategy may or may not be best for you, depending on your personal circumstances, but it is true that you'll probably incur significant health care expenses after you reach age 65. Being able to pay those costs with pre-tax money would be a significant benefit.

Chapter 7:
Required Minimum Distributions

100. Taking money from traditional IRAs

When you have a traditional IRA, there are two key milestones to keep in mind.

- **Age 59½.** Before then, you'll usually owe a 10% penalty on distributions, in addition to regular income tax. Some exceptions to this penalty apply, such as withdrawals for deductible medical expenses. Other retirement plans, such as 401(k)s, also incur this 10% surtax on early withdrawals, but the rules and the exceptions are not exactly the same as the IRA rules.

- **Age 72.** Now you must take required minimum distributions (RMDs) from your traditional IRA and, usually, from other retirement plans as well. However, if you are still working and own 5% or less of the company, you don't have to take RMDs from your current employer's retirement plan at that time, if the plan allows this. Additionally, if you own any qualifying longevity annuity contracts (QLACs) - a special type of retirement account annuity - you can delay RMDs until as late as the first day of the month after you turn 85. QLAC values are excluded from "regular" RMD calculations.

- If you were born on or after July 1, 1949, the 2019 retirement plan law (the SECURE Act) changed the RMD beginning age from 70½ to 72. If you were born before July 1, 1949, your first RMD year is still the year you turned 70½. You must continue taking RMDs for all subsequent years, and you do not get to delay RMDs until age 72.

What's more, if you have put money into a Roth IRA, you never have to take RMDs from that account, at any age.

- **Ed Slott's advice:** If you need the money, you can withdraw more than your RMD amount—it's a required minimum distribution. You can also take distributions from your IRAs at any age, but try to wait until you are at least 59½ to avoid the 10% penalty. If you must tap your IRA even earlier, ask your tax pro if there's a penalty exception you can use.

101. Time your RMDs correctly

You're usually required to take RMDs once you reach age 72, but that doesn't mean you must start exactly on your 72nd birthday. Technically, the deadline is April 1 of the year after the year you reach that magic age. The tax code manages the feat of turning one day into over a year!

Suppose Carol was born on July 1, 1949, so she didn't reach age 70½ until January 1, 2020. In this scenario, Carol gets the benefit of the new age 72 RMD rule and doesn't have to start RMDs until April 1 after the year she turns age 72 (April 1, 2022).

Subsequent RMDs are due the following December 31, and every December 31 after that. Carol, in our example, must take her first RMD by April 1, 2022, and her second RMD by December 31, 2022, less than nine months later. From then on, she must take her RMD by every December 31, as long as there is money in her IRA.

- **Ed Slott's advice:** You may not want to wait until April 1 to take your first RMD. If you do, you'll have two RMDs in the year you begin, and that "doubling up" might push you into a higher tax bracket.

Carol could have taken her first RMD in 2021, rather than wait until April 1, 2022. That will give her one taxable RMD per year and may allow her to stay in a lower tax bracket.

102. Calculate your RMD

The amount of your RMD generally depends on two things: your age and the amount in your IRA. Here's how you typically calculate it:

1. Look up the IRS Uniform Lifetime Table. You can find it at **irahelp.com/2021.**

2. Find your age as of December 31 of the year for which the RMD is due.

3. Find your life expectancy (in years).

4. Divide your life expectancy into your prior year-end account balance to find your RMD for the year.

In the previous example, Carol reached age 72 at the end of 2021 so she must take her first RMD by April 1, 2022. That's her RMD for 2021, the year in which she had her 72nd birthday. Thus, her first RMD will be determined by age 72 on this IRS table.

On the Uniform Lifetime Table, at age 72 an IRA participant has a life expectancy of 25.6 years. If Carol had $100,000 in her IRA on December 31, 2020, she would divide $100,000 by 25.6 to get $3,906: that's the RMD Carol must take by April 1, 2022.

103. Be leery of illiquid assets

Many investors have turned away from stocks (volatile) and bonds (low-yielding) in recent years. They might look for alternatives to hold in their IRAs, and IRS regulations permit many types of IRA investments, from real estate to private businesses.

- **The catch:** Stocks and bonds and other traded securities are easy to value for the purpose of determining RMDs. You simply look at the traded prices on December 31 of each relevant year.

That's not always the case with illiquid assets, such as the medical office building bought inside your IRA. Nevertheless, the IRS requires the IRA custodian to put a value on all IRA assets and RMDs must be calculated based on that value, after age 72. The cost of a valuation is paid by the IRA.

If the set value is too high, you'll withdraw too much from your IRA, pay too much in tax, and sacrifice untaxed wealth accumulation inside the account. However, if the set value is too low, you'll under-withdraw and take insufficient RMDs. This will expose you to a steep penalty, as explained below.

- **Ed Slott's advice:** If it's practical, consider eliminating hard-to-value assets from your IRA before age 72, so RMD valuation won't be an issue. Otherwise, consult with a tax pro to work out a valuation plan that will pass muster with the IRS.

104. Take your RMD—or else!

The R in RMD stands for Required, and the cost of ignoring this requirement is steep. Any shortfall is subject to a 50% penalty!

Suppose Carol has an initial $3,906 RMD, as illustrated prior. If she takes only $3,000 from her IRA by the deadline, Carol will be $906 below the minimum so she'll owe a $453 penalty: 50% of $906. If Carol takes no RMD at all, the penalty will be 50% of the entire $3,906 RMD, or $1,953.

Moreover, those are the penalty amounts. Carol is still required to take her missed RMD, and report the taxable income from her IRA distribution in the year in which she takes the distribution.

105. Let your custodian do the counting?

As you can imagine, determining your RMD can involve a substantial amount of number crunching. Any mistake might generate a too-small RMD and a 50% fine for any insufficient distribution.

IRA custodians are required to send out letters to IRA owners early each year, calculating their RMD for the year or offering to do so. However, using the number provided by the IRA custodian could be a mistake. The custodian will generally only use the date of birth they have on file for you and the Uniform Lifetime Table to calculate your RMD. If your spouse is more than 10 years younger or if your date of birth is wrong, the calculation they do for you will be wrong. It never hurts to double-check their math. After all, look where their math got them during the housing crisis!

- **Ed Slott's advice:** If you expect to use your RMD for spending money during the year, arrange with your custodian for monthly transfers from your IRA directly into your checking account. If that's not the case, waiting until year-end to take your annual RMD in a lump-sum will extend the time for potential tax-deferred buildup inside your IRA.

You should be aware that IRA custodians report to the IRS, too, so the tax collectors know who must withdraw from their IRAs. IRS may soon step up efforts to catch taxpayers who neglect this requirement to move money from one pocket to another.

ED SLOTT'S
ELITE
≡**IRA**≡
ADVISOR
GROUP™
Find an advisor
at **irahelp.com**

106. Mix and match IRA RMDs

Many people have more than one IRA. If so, you must calculate the RMD for each IRA to come up with your total RMD. Then you can take that RMD from any or all of your IRAs.

For example, suppose Art has one large IRA, another with $8,000 and yet another with $5,000. By adding up the RMDs from all three accounts, Art determines that he must take a total of $20,000 in RMDs this year.

Art decides to empty the two small IRAs, for a combined distribution of $13,000. Now, if he takes $7,000 from his large IRA, Art will have met his RMD for the year. Going forward, Art won't have to deal with paperwork from his two small IRAs; he will have only the large account, from which he will take all future RMDs.

If you have a SEP IRA or a SIMPLE IRA, you include that account among your IRAs when aggregating RMDs. However, you can't include inherited IRAs in that calculation—they need separate RMDs (more about inherited IRAs below). And you can't combine IRAs with employer plans for aggregating RMDs.

- **Ed Slott's advice:** Unless you have a special reason to keep multiple IRAs, consider consolidating them when you reach the RMD stage, or drawing down any small accounts. This will make your life simpler at age 72 and later years.

107. Don't take your spouse's RMD

Among married couples, both spouses may have their own IRAs. Thus, when both spouses are older than 72, they'll both have RMDs. Such couples should avoid a common error: taking all the RMDs from one spouse's IRA or IRAs.

Suppose that Grace has one IRA while her husband Joe has many IRAs, spread around several mutual fund companies. This year, Grace's RMD from her IRA is $18,000 while Joe's RMD total from all of his IRAs is $14,000.

Joe wants to take the $32,000 total RMD from his collection of IRAs, which will enable him to close out some IRAs and simplify his recordkeeping. After all, Joe reasons, the $32,000 of taxable IRA distributions will be reported on their joint tax return, so the couple will pay the proper amount of tax.

No harm, no foul….and no 50% penalty, Joe believes.

However, Joe is wrong. His reasoning will draw a yellow flag from the refs.

- **Ed Slott's advice:** The "I" in IRA stands for Individual. Each IRA owner should take RMDs from his or her own accounts. If not, the penalty will apply.

In the example above, Joe will have a $32,000 taxable distribution, drawing down his IRAs. Grace will have an $18,000 shortfall, and a 50% penalty ($9,000) for not taking her RMD. IRA beneficiaries also have RMDs, and aggregation rules to follow.

108. IRA beneficiaries have RMDs, too

As explained previously, IRA beneficiaries have certain rules to follow. In simplest terms:

- **Any IRA beneficiary** can withdraw all of the money from the account, and pay any resulting income tax. (Roth IRA beneficiaries often won't owe income tax.)

- **A surviving spouse who is an IRA beneficiary** can roll the IRA to his or her name. From there, the RMD rules apply as they apply to any IRA owner, starting at age 72.

- **All non-spouse IRA beneficiaries** not covered in the two points mentioned above are subject to RMD rules, even Roth IRA beneficiaries receiving tax-free distributions. Any RMD shortfall will trigger the 50% penalty.

- **Ed Slott's advice:** For maximum tax deferral, IRA beneficiaries (other than surviving spouses rolling over the account to their own name) should retitle the account to an inherited IRA. Typically, IRA custodians will have a preference as to the form of an inherited IRA's title.

109. The demise of the stretch IRA

If an IRA owner died before 2020, distributions to his or her named individual beneficiary could be spread out over the life expectancy of the beneficiary. This is called the "stretch IRA. "The stretch IRA allowed young beneficiaries to enjoy tremendous wealth building over many decades of tax deferral.

The 2019 retirement plan law (the SECURE Act) eliminated the stretch IRA for most heirs of IRA owners who die after December 31, 2019. Heirs of owners who died before January 1, 2020 can continue with their stretch IRA under the old rules.

110. Only "eligible designated beneficiaries" can use the stretch IRA

For deaths after December 31, 2019, only "eligible designated beneficiaries" can use the stretch IRA. Eligible designated beneficiaries are:

- Surviving spouses.
- Minor children (but not grandchildren).
- Disabled individuals (under a strict tax code definition).
- Chronically ill individuals.
- Beneficiaries no more than 10 years younger than the IRA owner.

Two points about eligible designated beneficiaries. First, whether you are eligible is determined on the date of the owner's death. Second, a minor child remains eligible until he or she reaches the age of majority (age 18 in most states) or while still in school up to age 26.

111. The new 10-year rule

If you are not an "eligible designated beneficiary" (e.g., a grandchild or older child), you must receive the entire IRA account by December 31 of the tenth year after the owner's death. No annual RMDs are required. You can decide to take any portion of the funds at any time within the 10-year period (or none at all), as long as the entire account is emptied by the end of the tenth year after death.

Suppose that Rick leaves his entire IRA account to his daughter, Amy, who is age 30. If Rick died before January 1, 2020, Amy could stretch her inherited IRA over her life expectancy by taking annual RMDs. However, if Rick dies after December 31, 2019, Amy is not an "eligible designated beneficiary." So, she does not have to take annual RMDs, but she must empty the account by no later than December 31 of the tenth year following Rick's death.

112. Calculating RMDs for "eligible designated beneficiaries"

To take RMDs from an inherited IRA, an "eligible designated beneficiary" (see tip #110) uses the IRS table found at **irahelp.com/2021**: the Single Life Expectancy Table. Generally, eligible designated beneficiaries look up their age in the year following the IRA owner's death.

Suppose, for example, that Nancy died in 2020 and left her $100,000 IRA to her minor child Phil. The first RMD is due by the end of 2021, the year of Phil's 15th birthday. On the IRS table, Phil has a life expectancy of 67.9 years, at age 15. Thus, Phil takes an RMD of $1,473 ($100,000 divided by 67.9) in December 2021.

Going forward, Phil reduces his life expectancy by one year, every year. In 2022, in our example, Phil's RMD will be based on a 66.9 life expectancy factor (67.9-1.0 = 66.9). If Phil stays in school until age 20, he must continue taking annual RMDs until that date. At that point, he is no longer an "eligible designated beneficiary" and can no longer stretch the inherited IRA by taking annual RMDs. Instead, he is now subject to the 10-year payout rule and must take the remaining IRA funds by no later than December 31 of the year he turns age 30.

113. Surviving spouses get extended life expectancy

Just to make things a little more complicated, the IRS has different rules for a surviving spouse who uses the same Single Life Expectancy Table to take RMDs from an inherited IRA—that is, for a surviving spouse who does not do a rollover to his or her own IRA.

As we saw with the Phil example above, non-spouse "eligible designated beneficiaries" have RMDs beginning in the year after death.

A surviving spouse, on the other hand, has no RMDs until the year their deceased spouse would have been age 72. On top of that, spousal beneficiaries who do have to take RMDs (because their deceased spouse would have already reached age 72) get to "recalculate" their life expectancy each year by looking up their life expectancy factor on the

Single Life Expectancy Table.

For example, let's suppose a spousal beneficiary has to take their first RMD in the year they turn age 55. Their factor, obtained from the Single Life Expectancy Table, is 29.6. The following year, the spousal beneficiary would, once again, look at the Single Life Expectancy Table, this time finding a factor of 28.7. The difference between these two factors is 0.9. In comparison, a non-spouse "eligible designated beneficiary" only looks at the table once – in the year after the IRA owner's death – and then subtracts one every year thereafter, resulting in a shorter life expectancy.

The longer life expectancy numbers used by surviving spouses produce smaller RMDs, smaller tax payments, and more potentially valuable tax deferral.

- **Ed Slott's advice:** Although most IRA beneficiaries who are surviving spouses will roll over the account to their own name, that's not always the case. A spouse beneficiary who will need to tap the IRA before age 59½ is often better off remaining as a beneficiary with an inherited IRA in order to avoid the 10% early withdrawal penalty.

  Once the survivor reaches age 59½, beyond that 10% penalty, he or she can roll over the IRA to his or her own name. Then they can defer RMDs until their age 72. There is no time limit on the ability of a surviving spouse to execute such an IRA rollover.

114. RMDs for multiple beneficiaries

Calculating the RMD when Mary leaves her IRA to her son John is relatively straightforward. If John is a minor child, he is considered an "eligible designated beneficiary." In that case, John (or his tax pro, or the IRA custodian) can go to the IRS life expectancy table for beneficiaries and do the math. But if John is an adult child, he must receive the entire IRA by December 31 of the tenth year after Mary's death.

But what if Mary leaves her IRA to her minor son John and her adult daughter Sue? In such a case, John will no longer be able to stretch his IRA while he remains a minor. Instead, both he and Sue must have their entire IRA shares paid by the end of the tenth year after Mary's death.

- **Ed Slott's advice:** In some situations, this rule is inconvenient and may become extremely costly for some heirs. Therefore, multiple IRA beneficiaries should mark their calendars to meet two key deadlines: September 30 of the year after the IRA owner dies and December 31 of the year after the IRA owner dies.

115. Determine the designated beneficiaries

By September 30 of the year after death, the "designated beneficiaries" will be determined. In some situations, acting before then can be helpful. For example:

- **When a charity or nonprofit organization** is among the IRA beneficiaries. Suppose Al's IRA had been left to his minor child, Craig, but it also included Al's alma mater as a beneficiary of 10%. A charity or nonprofit has no life expectancy so the IRA would have to be fully distributed in a relatively short time period. In that situation, Craig would lose some potentially valuable tax deferral inside the IRA.

  In this example, Craig can have the IRA custodian distribute 10% of the IRA account to the university, as payment in full. As long as the university is paid before September 30 of the year after the IRA owner's death, this will remove the college as a beneficiary, leaving only Craig as designated beneficiary. Then Craig can stretch RMDs, but only for awhile. The stretch must end when he reaches the age of majority or, if later, when he leaves school -- but in no case can the stretch extend beyond age 26. When the stretch ends, Craig's remaining funds must all be paid by the end of the tenth succeeding year.

116. Beneficiaries can go separate ways

If September 30 of the year after an IRA owner's death is the deadline for designating beneficiaries, what occurs three months later, on December 31? That's the deadline for separating an inherited IRA into multiple inherited IRAs, one for each beneficiary.

For example, imagine an IRA was left to the surviving spouse Barbara (50%), son Craig (25%), and daughter Diane (25%). Barbara rolled over her 50% share before the September 30 deadline, leaving Craig and Diane as co-beneficiaries of the IRA that remained. Assuming the IRA contained $400,000 at the owner's death, Craig and Diane would have an IRA worth $200,000.

Then, Craig and Diane would have until December 31 of that year to separate the account into two $100,000 inherited IRAs.

- **Ed Slott's advice:** By separating IRAs, each beneficiary gains more control over his or her own account because they can choose their own investments.

117. Trusts have their pros and cons

Some IRA owners name a trust as beneficiary. That is, when they die, their IRA will pass to a trust instead of to one or more individuals.

Example: When Edna Franklin fills out the beneficiary form for her IRA account, she enters "Franklin Family Trust" as her beneficiary. The trust document lists Edna's three children as the trust beneficiaries. A trustee is named who will manage the money inside the IRA after Edna dies and handle subsequent distributions.

- **Advantages:** Leaving your IRA (or any other asset) to a trust can be a good idea if you have an heir who is inexperienced in managing large amounts of money, is likely to squander the inheritance, or has other financial concerns. Suppose Edna's son Gregg bets (and loses heavily) on ball games, while her daughter Heather is a doctor, exposed to malpractice judgments. With a trust beneficiary, the IRA funds will be safer than if they had been left outright to Edna's children.

- **Drawbacks:** Any trust involves time and money to create and administer. In addition, because of the new rules under the 2019 retirement plan law (the SECURE Act), naming a trust as your IRA beneficiary is not necessarily a good idea. That's because, in most cases, either the trust beneficiaries or the trust itself will need to pay taxes on the entire IRA balance after 10 years following death. If you have such a trust in place, it will likely need to be revised or scrapped altogether. Contact your financial advisor and estate attorney right away!

118. Alternatives to IRA trusts

If you have a trust in place or are considering one, you should contact your estate attorney and financial advisor as soon as possible to discuss alternative planning strategies.

Name a spouse. One option is to simply name your spouse as beneficiary, since spouses (depending on their age) can have longer payout periods than an adult child or grandchild under the SECURE Act.

Convert to a Roth IRA. Roth conversions (see tips #11-13) are now especially important to reduce or eliminate the tax your heirs will have to pay within 10 years of your death.

Add life insurance. You may want to consider life insurance (see tips #43-50) as an estate and tax planning replacement for trusts.

Charitable trusts. If you are charitably-inclined and have a very large IRA, talk to your advisor or attorney about a charitable remainder trust (CRT).

119. Requesting RMD forgiveness

The previous items have focused on taking the right RMD amount from the right place and thus avoiding a 50% penalty. However, there might be circumstances in which you under-withdraw or just forget the RMD altogether. If that should happen, and you're facing a stiff fine, you can ask the IRS to waive the penalty. In order to succeed, you must demonstrate that the shortfall was due to a reasonable error and that you have taken the right actions to make up for your lapse.

You use IRS Form 5329, *Additional Taxes on Qualified Plans (Including IRAs) and Other Tax-Favored Accounts* to report the missed distribution and to calculate the penalty. To request a waiver, you must fill out the form and attach a letter of explanation.

Ed Slott's advice: When you submit Form 5329 with a statement requesting a waiver of the penalty, don't include payment for the 50% penalty. IRS no longer requires that payment be sent in with the form.

120. Making up missed RMDs

Before you file Form 5329 to request a waiver of the 50% penalty, you should actually take all the required distributions you've missed, as soon as you make the discovery of an RMD shortfall. Do the calculations, or have your tax professional do them, and move all the RMD amounts from your IRA to your taxable bank or investment account.

Suppose you missed a $10,000 RMD for 2018 and a $12,000 RMD for 2019. You should withdraw a total of $22,000 from any or all of your traditional IRAs in 2020, thus incurring $22,000 of taxable income for 2020.

- **Ed Slott's advice:** Assume that an IRS examiner will scrutinize your request for a penalty waiver. Therefore, you should do everything you can to help the IRS agent understand what you have done to correct your error.

  One possible approach is to ask your IRA custodian for separate checks that match each missed RMD. In the above example, you could ask your custodian for a $10,000 IRA distribution and a $12,000 distribution from your IRA with no taxes withheld. Make photocopies and then deposit the two checks into a taxable account.

121. File all necessary forms

If you owe penalties for multiple years, you must file a Form 5329 for each year in order to get a full waiver. These can be forms you file alone or ones that you file with an income tax return.

Previously, we gave the example of missed RMDs in 2018 and 2019. In such a situation, you should file two Forms 5329, one for each of those years. You can file a solo Form 5329 for 2018. If you have not yet filed your 2019 income tax return, you would attach Form 5329 for that year (or both years) to the tax return. Either way, attach a photocopy of the relevant distribution check to the Form 5329, showing that you have received that year's belated RMD from the IRA custodian.

- **Ed Slott's advice:** You shouldn't file an amended tax return as part of your request for a penalty waiver. Once you've missed an RMD for, say, 2018, you can't withdraw IRA money in 2020 and have it count for 2018. Instead, you'll take a makeup RMD in 2020, report that withdrawal on your 2020 tax return, and pay tax on that amount of income.

122. Conquering Form 5329

Requesting a waiver on Form 5329 doesn't require an advanced degree in computer science, but it's not child's play, either. Making a common mistake can be costly.

The danger lies in Part VIII of the form, labeled "Additional Tax on Excess Accumulation in Qualified Retirement Plans (Including IRAs)." Here's how to sidestep the trap:

- **On line 52,** enter the amount of the RMD that you were required to take.
- **On line 53,** enter the total of IRA distributions that you actually took during that calendar year.
- **On line 54,** enter "zero," and write "RC" (for reasonable cause) in the margin. Do not enter the amount of the RMD you missed.
- **On line 55,** enter "zero" again.
- **Ed Slott's advice:** The instructions for line 54 of Form 5329 can be confusing, but you should be sure not to put any number on that line. If you put any amount there, you won't get the waiver you're requesting. Instead, the IRS will impose the 50% penalty tax and request payment in full.

123. State your case for a penalty waiver

When you file Form 5329, requesting a waiver of the 50% penalty for a missed RMD, be sure to attach a waiver request. Emphasize that you have taken an IRA distribution equal to the missed RMD, as evidenced by the attached copy of the distribution check from your IRA custodian.

Your statement also should include an explanation for missing the RMD. Unfortunately, the IRS has not issued any notices or rulings that would indicate what's considered to be a good reason for getting a penalty waiver.

- **Ed Slott's advice:** Just saying "I forgot" is not likely to get the penalty dismissed. You'll need to show a reasonable cause. Here are some explanations that the IRS might accept:

  1. Illness or death in the family.

  2. Failure on the part of your IRA custodian, which didn't inform you of your RMD.

  3. Failure on the part of the Post Office, so notices about RMDs never reached you.

  4. Problems with a reputable tax preparer.

  5. Exceptional stress, which might involve a divorce, a lost job, a home foreclosure, the closing of a family business, etc.

In any event, your statement should apologize for the inadvertent oversight, point out that the missed RMDs have been taken, and promise to make every attempt to make all future RMDs on time.

124. Charitable thoughts about RMDs

RMDs generate unwelcome taxes, but a missed RMD generates a steep penalty, and there is no sure way to have that penalty waived. What's more, taking an RMD inflates your adjusted gross income (AGI), and a higher AGI can have expensive consequences throughout your tax return. Just to name a couple of examples, a higher AGI can cost you medical deductions and prevent you from deducting losses from investment property.

- **Now for the good news:** Fortunately, there is a way to satisfy your RMD requirement without getting snared by all these tax traps. You can utilize a tax break called a qualified charitable distribution (QCD). Here's how it works:

Suppose Ellen is 75 years old, with an RMD from her traditional IRA of $20,000 this year. Ellen, who is charitably inclined, chooses to transfer $20,000 from her IRA to her favorite charity this year. That $20,000 can be a QCD, satisfying her RMD and absolving her from the 50% penalty. It's true that Ellen won't get the usual tax deduction for this charitable donation, but it's also true that Ellen won't have to include that $20,000 distribution in her AGI, and that exclusion can have multiple tax-saving benefits.

QCDs are especially valuable to seniors who (a) have an IRA and (b) take the standard deduction on their tax return, so they don't deduct charitable contributions. Such IRA owners get no tax benefit from their donations so they might as well make them from their IRA and avoid the taxable income from their RMDs.

125. Breaking down the QCD tax break

Now that the QCD is a permanent part of the tax code, it's even more important to know how to make one properly. Here's what you need to know:

- You have to be at least age 70½ as of the date of the transfer to use the tax break. Beneficiaries over age 70½ are also eligible.

- QCDs can count as RMDs, but QCDs can be made in amounts higher than the RMD (up to the annual limit) or even in years when no RMD is due.

- The annual limit is $100,000 of QCDs per donor, so a couple in that age range can donate up to $200,000 ($100,000 each) from their respective IRAs.

- Your IRA custodian must make a payment to the charity or charities you designate, not to you. Public charities and nonprofit organizations (colleges and museums, for instance) generally are acceptable recipients.

- Donations to a donor-advised fund, a private foundation, or a supporting organization won't be acceptable as a QCD.

- The charitable recipient must receive your name and address, so it can send you the required acknowledgment. This letter should state that it received the money and did not provide you with any benefit in return.

- **Ed Slott's advice:** If you make a deductible IRA contribution in the same year you take a QCD, a portion of your QCD may be taxable. For this reason, you may be better off making a Roth IRA contribution.

Chapter 8:

2021
Tax Update

The SECURE Act Makes Fundamental Changes to IRA Tax Planning

The ***Setting Every Community Up for Retirement Enhancement Act of 2019 (the SECURE Act)*** was signed into law by President Trump on December 20, 2019 as part of the Consolidated Appropriations Act, 2020. Earlier chapters of this guide discussed several of the key SECURE Act changes:

- Elimination of the "stretch IRA" for most beneficiaries. For deaths after December 31, 2019, only "eligible designated beneficiaries" (surviving spouses, minor children, disabled individuals, chronically ill individuals and beneficiaries not more than 10 years younger than the IRA owner) can still use the stretch IRA. Other named individual beneficiaries must receive their entire inherited IRA by December 31 of the tenth year following the IRA owner's death. (See tips #109-112 for more details.)

- Extension of the first RMD to age 72. If you were born on or after July 1, 1949, your first required minimum distribution (RMD) year is extended from age 70½ to age 72.

- Elimination of the age 70½ limit for traditional IRA contributions. Beginning in 2020, if you are age 70½ or older, you can make traditional IRA contributions – as long as you have compensation or earned income. (See tip #6 for more details.)

- Penalty-free withdrawals for birth or adoption. Even if you are under age 59½, you can make penalty-free withdrawals from your IRA after birth or adoption. (See tip #75 for more details.)

Other Provisions of Interest

- Graduate or postdoctoral students can now make IRA contributions on taxable payments of fellowships and stipends.
- Foster care workers can now make nondeductible IRA contributions and after-tax contributions to company savings plans on nontaxable "difficulty of care" payments.
- The "multiple employer plan" rules have been relaxed to make it easier for unrelated companies to band together to offer retirement plans.
- Section 529 plans can now be used to cover costs associated with certain apprenticeships and up to $10,000 of student loan repayments.
- The threshold for itemizing medical expenses is lowered from 10% to 7.5% of adjusted gross income for 2019 and 2020.

Tax Cuts and Jobs Act Makes Major Changes

On December 22, 2017, the **Tax Cuts and Jobs Act** was signed into law. This far-reaching piece of legislation overhauled the tax code. What does it all mean for you and your retirement plan? Here are some highlights.

Big Changes!

Tax reform kept seven tax brackets and lowered the top rate to 37% for individuals. The alternative minimum tax (AMT) has been scaled way back. The standard deduction is now $12,550 in 2021 for singles and $25,100 for those who are married, filing jointly, and the child credit has been expanded. Personal exemptions are suspended.

Many popular deductions have been eliminated or scaled back. The state and local tax deduction is limited to $10,000, and the mortgage interest deduction will be limited to the first $750,000 in mortgage interest debt for new home purchases.

These changes, like most of the changes tax reform brings for individuals, are scheduled to sunset after 2025. Tax reform also brought sweeping reform to corporate taxation. Changes on the corporate side, unlike the individual side, are permanent.

Your Retirement Plan

When it comes to your retirement plan, the big news may be what was NOT changed by tax reform.

Your ability to make pretax salary deferrals to your 401(k) is unchanged.

Proposals to require after-tax contributions, instead of pre-tax (i.e., the so called "Rothification" concept), never made it into the final legislation.

Roth IRA conversions may make more sense than ever.

Tax brackets have been lowered and the AMT has been limited to a very few taxpayers. This may be the time to have a conversation about conversion with your advisor. These changes are currently scheduled to sunset in a few years, so there is a window of opportunity here. Now may be the time to act. No one knows for sure what the future will bring, but higher tax rates are a strong possibility. Converting now locks in today's low rates and avoids the worries of future tax uncertainty.

Recharacterization of Roth IRA conversions is not available for conversions done in 2018 or later.

Conversions are now irrevocable. A Roth conversion may still be the right strategy for you, but you must be sure. You will want to be certain that there is enough money available outside of your IRA to pay the taxes. Because there is no "do-over," advice from a knowledgeable advisor is more important than ever. Doing smaller, or partial, conversions to hedge your bets may be a strategy worth undertaking. Also, waiting until closer to the end of the year when you have a better understanding of your tax situation may be a wise move.

Recharacterization of contributions survives.

This is good news for those who change their mind about the type of IRA to which they want to contribute. For example, if you discover your traditional IRA contribution is not deductible, you can still recharacterize that contribution to a Roth IRA if you are eligible to make a Roth contribution for the year.

Consider a back-door Roth IRA if your income is too high for you to make Roth IRA contributions.

If you had concerns about this tactic in the past, you can rest easy. The committee reports that were released along with the new law explicitly mentioned the tactic on four separate occasions. However, you must have taxable compensation. Also, the pro-rata formula will apply.

Qualified charitable distributions (QCDs) are more valuable than ever.

The QCD has always been a great tool for those who have an IRA and are charitably-minded. With tax reform expanding the standard deduction and doing away with many popular deductions, it is expected that fewer taxpayers than ever will itemize their deductions. This means that even though the charitable deduction remains, fewer taxpayers will use it. A QCD is a way you can still get a tax break for your charitable contribution while also using the new expanded standard deduction. If you are over 70½, you can transfer up to $100,000 tax-free directly from your IRA to the qualifying charity of your choice. These funds will not be included in your income for the year, and you can even use a QCD to satisfy your RMD.

Tax reform does away with the itemized deduction for advisory fees for your IRA.

Consider paying these fees directly from your traditional IRA instead of out of pocket. Although it reduces the amount growing tax-deferred, you get a break by using pretax dollars. Because Roth IRAs are an after-tax account, this strategy won't work there.

Tax reform also does away with your ability to claim a loss on your IRA.

This was only available if you cashed out all your IRAs of the same type and the total distribution was less than your basis, so it was uncommon. However, now it is eliminated.

You will have more time to roll over a plan loan offset if you leave your job or the plan is terminated.

Old rules only gave you sixty days to roll over the unpaid loan balance. Tax reform will extend this rollover deadline until your tax return due date (including extensions) for the year during which the loan offset occurred. This can help if you are between jobs and need more time to come up with the cash.

Bipartisan Budget Act of 2018 Impacts Retirement Plans

On February 9, 2018, President Trump signed the Bipartisan Budget Act of 2018 (BBA) into law. While the new law is best known for keeping the government open, it also includes some provisions that impact retirement plans.

Hardship Distribution Rule Changes

The BBA made some direct changes to the hardship distribution rules. These changes are effective January 1, 2020.

- **Elimination of the Six-Month Prohibition on Contributions:** Under prior law, once a participant received a hardship distribution, he or she was prohibited from making contributions to the plan for six months. This six-month prohibition is no longer required or allowed.

- **Expansion of Eligible Hardship Distribution Funds:** The BBA also expands the types of retirement funds that are eligible for a hardship distribution. Currently, the employee can only receive a hardship distribution of his or her elective salary deferral contributions. Under the BBA, hardship distributions will include any qualified non-elective contributions, qualified matching contributions and the earnings on salary deferral contributions.

- **No Longer the Last Resort:** The BBA also eliminates the rule that required participants to take plan loans before accessing hardship distributions.

Rollover of Wrongful Levy

If the IRS wrongfully levies a retirement plan or IRA and returns those funds (plus interest) to the taxpayer, the BBA allows the taxpayer to roll over the amount received to a retirement plan or IRA. The rollover must be completed by the individual's tax filing due date for the year in which the funds are returned. This deadline does not include any extensions. The new law applies to levied funds returned to a taxpayer in tax years beginning after December 31, 2017. The rollover does not count for purposes of the one-rollover-per-year rule.

Your Estate Plan

The estate, gift and generation skipping tax exemptions are increased to $23,400,000 (married couple) or $11,700,000 per person for 2021.

The top rate stays at 40%, and the step-up in basis stays intact. But these changes are only through the end of 2025, and then the exemptions go back to the $5 million per person indexed for inflation. With such high exemptions available, few estates will be hit with the estate tax. However, those that are subject to the tax will be hit hard. If that is you, talk to your advisor about strategies such as maximizing gifts over the next few years. When planning, don't overlook the state estate tax, which can have much lower exemptions than the newly increased federal ones.

Education Savings

529 plans have been expanded. Previously, these accounts could only be used for higher education expenses. Now, 529 accounts can distribute up to $10,000 annually per student to pay for public, private, or religious primary or secondary school costs.

Contribution limits have been increased for ABLE accounts.

If you have family members with disabilities, tax reform brings some good news in the form of increased contribution limits. Also, the designated beneficiary of the ABLE account can claim the Saver's Credit for contributions made to their account. The Saver's Credit was previously only available for retirement plan contributions.

Distributions from 529 plans can now be rolled over to an ABLE account, if that ABLE account is owned by the designated beneficiary of that 529 account or a family member.

Rollovers count towards the annual contribution limit.

Other Provisions of Interest

- The Affordable Care Act's individual mandate, which penalizes people who do not have health care, went away in 2019.

- In the past, taxpayers could claim a deduction for major losses arising from fire, storm, or similar casualties, with some limitations. Tax reform will restrict this. Personal casualty losses will be deductible only if the losses are due to a federally declared disaster. If you are not in a federally declared disaster area, casualty losses will no longer be deductible.

- The corporate tax rate was cut from 35% to 21% starting in 2018. The AMT for corporations has been eliminated. Tax reform also creates a 20% business income deduction with some limits for pass-through businesses such as partnerships and shareholders of S-corporations, LLCs and partnerships. Unlike the majority of the tax cuts for individuals under tax reform, these changes for businesses are permanent. Now may be a good time to investigate changing your business structure to maximize your benefits under the new rules.

Good Advice Is Essential

Do you have questions about your own situation? These big changes mean that now more than ever, good advice is essential. A qualified financial advisor can help guide you through all the new rules and ensure that you are best positioned to take advantage of the breaks and avoid the pitfalls.

Overview of the 2021 Tax Rates

Taxable Income Brackets for 2021 Ordinary Income Tax Rates

Marginal Tax Rate	Married Filing Joint	Single
10%	$0 -$19,900	$0 - $9,950
12%	$19,901-$81,050	$9,951-$40,525
22%	$81,051-$172,750	$40,526-$86,375
24%	$172,751-$329,850	$86,376-$164,925
32%	$329,851-418,850	$164,926-$209,425
35%	$418,851-$628,300	$209,426-$523,600
37%*	$628,301 or more	$523,601 or more

* The top rate is effectively 40.8% for those subject to the 3.8% Medicare surtax on net investment income.

Capital Gains and Qualified Dividends

The top tax rate for long-term capital gains and dividends remains at 20%.

2021 Capital Gains Tax Brackets:

Married filing jointly	
$0 - $80,800	0%
$80,801- $501,600	15%*
$501,601 or more	20%**

Single	
$0 - $40,400	0%
$40,401-$445,850	15%*
$445,851 or more	20%**

*Some of those in the 15% capital gains bracket will pay 18.8% if they are subject to the 3.8% net investment income tax.

**In nearly all cases the 20% capital gains rate will be 23.8%, after adding the 3.8% net investment income tax, which applies at lower income amounts.

Trust tax rates reach the 20% capital gains tax rate after $13,250 of taxable income.

2021 Trust Tax Rates

10%	$0 - $2,650
24%	$2,651-$9,550
35%	$9,551-$13,050
37%	$13,051 or more

Estate Tax

The exemptions for estate, gift and generation skipping tax in 2021 are now up to $11,700,000.

The top rate is 40%

2021 Estate & Gift Exemption Amounts	
Estate Tax	$11,700,000
Generation Skipping Tax	$11,700,000
Gift Tax	$11,700,000
Annual Gift Tax Exclusion	$15,000

Estate Tax Portability

The portability feature for the estate and gift tax exemptions is now permanent, providing married couples with a total exemption of up to $23,400,000.

The estate tax return, Form 706, must be filed to get portability of a deceased spouse's remaining exemption.

There is no portability of the generation skipping transfer (GST) tax exemption.

ABOUT ED SLOTT

Ed Slott is a nationally recognized IRA distribution expert, professional speaker, television personality, and best-selling author. He is known for his unparalleled ability to turn advanced tax strategies into understandable, actionable and entertaining advice. He has been named "The Best Source for IRA Advice" by *The Wall Street Journal*, and *USA Today* wrote, "It would be tough to find anyone who knows more about IRAs than CPA Slott."

As president and founder of Ed Slott and Company, LLC, the nation's leading source of accurate, timely IRA expertise and analysis to financial advisors, institutions, consumers and media, he provides:

1. Advanced training to financial professionals to become knowledgeable recognized leaders in the retirement marketplace; and

2. Answers to retirement savers' most important questions, continually providing practical, easy-to-understand information on IRA, retirement, tax and financial planning topics.

Mr. Slott is a Professor of Practice at The American College of Financial Services and regularly presents on IRA and estate planning strategies at both consumer events and conferences for financial advisors, insurance professionals, CPAs and attorneys, including virtual events drawing thousands of attendees nationwide. He has provided topical keynote presentations for leading financial membership organizations, including the Financial Planning Association, National Association of Personal Financial Advisors, Estate Planning Councils and the American Institute of Certified Public Accountants, as well as leading corporate financial firms coast-to-coast. He is also the creator of Ed Slott's Elite IRA Advisor GroupSM, an organization of more than 400 of the nation's top financial professionals who attend his ongoing continuing-education programs to maintain a mastery of advanced retirement account and tax planning laws.

Mr. Slott is an accomplished author of many financial and retirement-focused books, including most recently *Ed Slott's Retirement Decisions Guide: 2021 Edition* (IRAHelp, 2021) and *Fund Your Future: A Tax-Smart Savings Plan in Your 20s and 30s* (IRAHelp, 2021) with *The New Retirement Savings Time Bomb* (Penguin Random House, 2021). He also hosts the popular website **irahelp.com** as a resource for financial professionals and consumers, where The Slott Report blog is followed by tens of thousands of readers.

As the go-to resource for media on timely insight on breaking news as it relates to retirement and tax planning laws and strategies, Mr. Slott is often quoted in *The New York Times*, *The Wall Street Journal*, *Forbes*, *USA Today*, *Kiplinger*, *Investor's Business Daily* and numerous additional national magazines and financial publications. He provides a monthly Q&A column to AARP and is also a contributing columnist and media resource to Financial Planning, Financial Advisor and InvestmentNews magazines. He has appeared on many national television and radio programs, including *NBC, ABC, CBS, CNBC, CNN, FOX, FOXBUSINESS, NPR, Bloomberg* and *Morningstar*. He is one of the top pledge drivers of all time with his educational specials, including his most recent, *"Retire Safe & Secure! with Ed Slott" (2021).*

Mr. Slott is a past Chairman of the New York State Society of CPAs Estate Planning Committee and editor of the IRA planning section of the *CPA Journal*. He was named a 2020 *InvestmentNews* Innovator for his significant contribution to helping advisors improve client outcomes and tackle industry challenges as well as the 2020 Sidney Kess Award Winner for excellence in continuing education by the AICPA®. He is also the recipient of the prestigious "Excellence in Estate Planning" and "Outstanding Service" awards presented by The Foundation for Accounting Education. He is a former board member of The Estate Planning Council of New York City and is Accredited Estate Planner (AEP) distinguished.

Ultimately, through all of these efforts combined, Mr. Slott has taught millions of Americans (and their financial professionals) how to get the most out of their retirement savings.

"The Best Source of IRA Advice"
— The Wall Street Journal

For more information:

Website: irahelp.com

Email: info@irahelp.com

Twitter: @theslottreport

Facebook: AmericasIRAExperts

LinkedIn: Ed Slott and Company

YouTube: EdSlottandCompanyIRA

Notes

10 Questions to Ask Your Financial Advisor

1. I know this area requires specialized knowledge in IRA distribution planning. Do you have expertise in this area? How would I know that?

2. What books have you read on the topic? Look at the books. If they crack when you open them..run. It's the first time the book has been opened.

3. What professional training do you take in IRA distribution planning? What courses or programs have you taken? Can you show me the last course manual you received?

4. How do you stay current on key IRA tax laws, such as the SECURE Act? What services or resources do you rely on to stay up to date? Can you show me a sample?

5. What is the latest IRA tax rule you are aware of? When did it occur?

6. How do you determine the best option for my lump-sum distribution? What are all of my choices?

7. How would you keep track of my IRA beneficiary form? When should I update my IRA beneficiary form? What are the key events that would trigger a need for a review?

8. Can you show me the IRS life expectancy tables?

9. Do you know what will happen to my IRA after I die?

10. Who do YOU turn to when you have questions on IRA distribution planning? No one can know it all.